Doing a systematic literature review

Doing a systematic literature review in legal scholarship

Marnix Snel
Janaína de Moraes

eleven

international publishing

Published, sold and distributed by Eleven International Publishing
P.O. Box 85576
2508 CG The Hague
The Netherlands
Tel.: +31 70 33 070 33
Fax: +31 70 33 070 30
e-mail: sales@elevenpub.nl
www.elevenpub.com

Sold and distributed in USA and Canada
International Specialized Book Services
920 NE 58th Avenue, Suite 300
Portland, OR 97213-3786, USA
Tel: 1-800-944-6190 (toll-free)
Fax: +1-503-280-8832
orders@isbs.com
www.isbs.com

Eleven International Publishing is an imprint of Boom uitgevers Den Haag.

ISBN 978-94-6236-807-1
NUR 820

© 2018 Marnix Snel and Janaína de Moraes | Eleven International Publishing

Printed in the Netherlands

Table of Contents

1 Introduction

1.1 Focus of this book

In short, a literature review is the comprehensive study and interpretation of literature that relates to a particular topic (Aveyard, 2010, p. 5). Such a study is undertaken with two different aims in mind. Firstly, a literature review may serve as a preliminary – and we believe necessary – investigation prior to embarking on a larger academic research venture. The main purpose here is to provide a critical account of the literature in a particular area in order to demonstrate why a new study is required. In other words, to *embed* and *justify* a proposed research question. Secondly, a literature review may form the entire academic project. In this case, the literature is reviewed in order to *answer* a particular question.[1]

In this book, we will focus on the literature review in the former sense, that is, as the first step in a bigger study. We want to emphasize the (often-underestimated) importance of conducting a systematic literature review at the start of an academic legal research project[2] (**chapter 2**) and introduce the basic steps we deem necessary in order to successfully complete it. We move consecutively through the process of delineating your topic and determining the information to search for (**chapter 3**), designing and carrying out a systematic search for relevant literature (**chapter 4**), critically appraising the literature (**chapter 5**), and synthesizing, discussing and presenting your findings (**chapter 6**).

Before we proceed to that, we find it important to address briefly why we think the construction of this book was necessary for the legal discipline (*paragraph 1.2*), to present the methods we followed to reach our findings (*paragraph 1.3*), and to provide some information on how we think this book should be used by our intended audience (*paragraph 1.4*). We sincerely hope this book helps those undertaking academic legal research to overcome existing insecurities and that it, mod-

---

1   An example of this is Meuwese & Snel's '*Constitutional Dialogue: An Overview*' (2014). Cooper (1998) emphasizes that a literature review that "appears independent of new data" can serve many different purposes.

2   Our understanding of academic legal research is a broad one. We not only consider it to include more traditional forms of legal scholarship – doctrinal legal research, comparative law, legal history, and legal theory/jurisprudence – but also the more interdisciplinary forms of legal research that have evolved over the years – socio-legal, law and economics, empirical legal studies, et cetera – see *paragraph 3.3* and *paragraph 3.4*.

estly but still, contributes to the efficiency of your research trajectory and the quality of your thesis.

1.2   Why this book?

Legal scholarship is a discipline in transition (Van Gestel, Micklitz, & Maduro, 2012, pp. 12-19). One of the structural changes legal scholarship is undergoing is an increasing focus on legal research methodology. As a result, the body of literature on legal research methods has grown strongly over the past years.[3] Several of these contributions come to the – in our view, right – conclusion that the performance of a comprehensive preliminary investigation is a prerequisite for both the construction of a solid research proposal[4] *and* the efficient and auspicious realization thereof (Epstein & King, 2002, p. 59; Samuel, 2014, pp. 26-27; Snel, 2017b; Vranken, 2014, pp. 59-60).[5] What we did not find though, is the necessary elaboration of how exactly that might take place.

We believe that we cannot expect novice legal scholars to execute a preliminary investigation in a meaningful way without providing them with at least some written guidelines on how to do so (best combined with courses by librarians and researchers who have experience in carrying out a systematic literature review[6]). The activity at stake is simply too complex to be learned by trial and error during the course of a single (or even a few) research project(s).[7] Especially if one realizes that, because of globalization and digitalization of both legal scholarship and the law itself, the body of research materials at the disposal of the legal scholar has become larger and more obscure than ever before.[8]

While guidelines on how to do a literature review in legal scholarship are missing, one could argue that the legal scholar in search of information on how to do a systematic literature review only has to reach beyond the boundaries of her discipline. We, however, sincerely believe that legal scholarship should not *and* cannot

---

3   For textbooks, see for instance Cahillane and Schweppe (2016) and Hanson (2016). For dissertations, see Tijssen (2009, with English summary), Kestemont (2016) summarized in English in Kestemont (2015), and Snel (2016, English version forthcoming).

4   Moreover, in many countries, the literature review has become a standard element of research proposals required by research funding agencies.

5   Snel (2017a) distinguishes between preliminary research aimed at (*1*) the state of knowledge on a given subject, (*2*) the construction of a research framework, and (*3*) assessing the feasibility of the research project through a pilot study. In this book, we confine ourselves to the first type of preliminary research.

6   Also proposed by, for instance, Davidson (2010), Osborne (2016), and Drake (2016).

7   Also take into consideration the fact that empirical research has revealed that students and postgraduates (including those studying law) often overestimate their own information and research skills, including their ability to retrieve relevant literature on a particular topic. See for instance Barry (1997), Green and Macauley (2007), and Osborne (2012).

8   We have not only noticed a rise in sheer numbers, but also in 'new' source-types such as blogs – blawgs –, unpublished papers, reports, Wikipedia pages, et cetera.

rely merely on guidelines developed in other disciplines. While that literature may serve as a welcome source of inspiration (as it did for us, see *paragraph 1.3*), we emphasize that the exact way in which a literature review is carried out are, in the end, (too) discipline-dependent. Legal information systems do not function in the same way as the *Cumulative Index to Nursing and Allied Health Literature* does, the close connection that exists between legal scholarship and legal practice results in a distinction between academic, professional and popular publications which is uncommon in most other disciplines (Stolker, 2014, pp. 207-210), and so on.

Seen in conjunction, this has led to our belief that the creation of this book was necessary. We believe it is high time to develop some guidelines for doing a systematic literature review that are specific to legal scholarship; that we provide our young scholars with both an alternative to learning on the job and an opportunity to benchmark the practices they have evolved themselves.

1.3   How this book was compiled

We established the guidelines we present in this book by conducting a systematic literature review *on* the systematic literature review ourselves. A search in the most important databases and on the open web quickly showed us that there is an abundance of contributions from scholars operating in various disciplines (in all shapes and sizes) that deal with our topic.[9] As it was impossible to consult and incorporate the insights from all of these materials, we decided to focus on published textbooks and journal articles in the disciplines of medicine, social science and humanities[10] which actually propose *techniques* that may be employed when engaging in a systematic review of the relevant literature on a particular topic.

Where necessary, we translated what we found so that it would fit the specific characteristics of legal scholarship and added clarifying examples.[11] To ensure the

---

9   Apart from published works, we also came across several unpublished papers, policy documents, course manuals, websites, instruction videos, and so on. Not all of them use the term 'literature review'. As Cooper (1998) and Garrad (2011) remarked, there are many terms that are sometimes used interchangeably to label similar activities, including 'research review', 'integrative research review', 'research synthesis', and 'meta-analysis'.

10   This is motivated by the fact that the relevant literature is particularly well-developed in these disciplines (also remarked by Baude, Chilton, & Malani, 2017, p. 45; Cooper, 1998).

11   We noticed that we were not the first to do so. Dobinson and Johns (2007, pp. 22-32) used Fink's '*Conducting research literature review: from the internet to paper*' to design a method for identifying relevant legislation, cases and secondary materials in law. Baude et al. (2017) argued for the development of methods for performing systematic reviews that are specifically tailored to legal analysis. What these contributions have in common is that they use the insights from the books and papers on the systematic literature review to present lessons on how to *answer* a legal research question, thus – in our conception – ignoring an important lesson: that the systematic literature review is first and foremost necessary to *find* and *develop* an academic research question. This, however, does not mean that their translations were not useful to us. On

correctness of our translations, we drew upon the scarce and fragmented *legal* literature that addresses certain aspects of the literature review (have other legal scholars proposed techniques that are similar to those we developed by translating the insights from other academic disciplines?).[12] The examples added were mainly extricated from the experience we have with both the drafting and assessment (in the context of research proposals for dissertations and students' theses) of systematic literature reviews.

1.4   How to use this book

This book was written with, in particular, two groups of readers in mind. Primarily, it is aimed at undergraduates who are engaging in academic research (including a bachelor's and/or master's thesis) as part of the requirement for their degree program. We, however, sincerely believe that more experienced researchers (especially doctoral students, but also more seasoned researchers) may also benefit from the insights we provide in this book.

We would like to warn our readers of the fact that the straightforwardness of this book may lead to an underestimation of the difficulties that may be encountered when doing a systematic literature review. We believe this will change, however, as soon as the reader applies what she has learned to the practice of her own research. Only then will it become clear that the distinct steps of the literature review are more difficult than they may at first appear. Therefore, after finishing each chapter, the reader is encouraged to apply the suggestions to her own research project. Be aware, though, that in reality the different steps may overlap and/or require mutual input (compare Wisker, 2015, p. 64).[13] This means – and we will repeat this regularly – that you will have to go back and forth a lot between the different steps we propose.[14]

Perhaps superfluously, we would like to add that applying the methodology in this book to an actual research project will not automatically guarantee the quality of the literature review. Doing research comprises much more than simply follow-

---

the contrary. These works provided inspiration, concrete insights and examples that we were able to use for our purpose here.

12   Legal publications that, for instance, provide an overview of databases where source materials can be found and how to search these databases.

13   For instance, when critically appraising the literature, you may come across an interesting association with your topic that you did not anticipate. This might mean that you have to go back to the step where you designed your search process to enable you to include the literature that relates to your association, see *paragraph 5.5*.

14   Even after you have finished (the first version of) your literature review. See Bryman (2008, p. 83), who stated: "[b]ear in mind that reading the literature is not something that you should stop doing once you begin designing your research. You should continue your search for and reading of relevant literature more or less throughout your research. This means that, if you have written a literature review before beginning your data collection, you will need to regard it as provisional. Indeed, you may want to make quite substantial revisions of your review towards the end of writing up your work".

ing a list of technical procedures (Barbour, 2001, p. 1115; Fisher, Lange, Scotford, & Carlarne, 2009, p. 227). Although we profoundly believe that the guidelines we provide can contribute to the quality and efficiency of your research, we recognize that the quality of that research is ultimately dependent on a combination of being systematic *and* elements like integrity, talent, intuition, creativity, imagination, perseverance, analytical capacity, and even coincidence or luck (Cook & Campbell, 1979; Poincare, 1913).

> On a final introductory note, we want to mention that while this book specifically focuses on the literature review as a preliminary investigation for a research project, the insights provided are, of course, also relevant for the situation where the literature review forms the entire project.

2 What is a literature review and why do one?

2.1 Introduction

Undertaking a systematic literature review is time-consuming. We therefore believe it is important that you first understand *why* you should invest a substantial portion of your research time in reviewing the literature to *find* a question rather than just quickly pose and start *answering* one. Moreover, appreciating the motives for doing a literature review will enable you to fully grasp what a systematic literature review comprises (we will summarize it for you in *paragraph 2.7* and *paragraph 2.8*) and, perhaps even more crucially, make you realize that (and how) going through the different steps we propose in this book may contribute to the effectiveness and quality of your entire research project.

You should be aware of the fact that each research enterprise consists of three global stages (Fajans & Falk, 2011; Verschuren & Doorewaard, 2010, pp. 16-24): (*1*) determining your area of interest (*topic choice*) (*2*) phrasing, embedding, and planning how to realize your research objective(s) and question(s) (constructing your *conceptual* and *technical* research design),[1] and (*3*) answering your research question(s) (*implementation phase*). We will first explain where *exactly* the literature review is located in this three-step process, as this will help you understand why executing a systematic literature review is necessary to get through your entire research project smoothly (*paragraph 2.2*).

We will then go into the four different reasons why doing a literature review is indispensable. Firstly, reviewing the literature will help you to *really* understand your topic and the field it is in (*paragraph 2.3*). Secondly, doing a literature review will allow you to narrow down your topic to researchable proportions (*paragraph 2.4*). Thirdly, the literature review is indispensable for embedding your research question and justifying why answering it is worth the time investment (*paragraph 2.5*). Finally, a literature review may help you estimate how best to answer your research question and whether that can be done in the time that is reserved for your project (*paragraph 2.6*).

---

1   The conceptual design involves determining everything you wish to achieve through the project; the technical design is concerned with the development of a set of activities for realizing all this during the implementation stage (Verschuren & Doorewaard, 2010, p. 16).

2.2   Interaction between topic choice and literature review

When you stand before a research task, you have to start somewhere. For most students, doing research starts with the determination of an area that interests them. While that may sound simple, it is, in fact, a high hurdle for many students. According to Meeker (1996, p. 917), "[t]he student of law, commanded to find a research topic, is faced with a daunting chicken-and-egg problem – the student must do a great deal of research to assess a topic on which to do research". In our view, a distinction must be made between two types of research you must do to assess a topic to research. Firstly, there is the research you do that leads to the first encounter with a (mostly, but not necessarily, still quite general) topic that may be worth pursuing. Secondly, there is the research you do to, from there, come to an actually researchable academic research question.

We would say that the adage for the research you do to get on the track of a possible research topic, is 'anything goes'.[2] You might start by browsing through recent law journals, looking for new developments (a new legislative proposal, for instance, or a new phenomenon – *i.e.* self-driving cars, Airbnb, Uber, et cetera – that raises questions that are legally relevant), going through the most recent decisions of the Supreme Court or other courts (the court introduced a seemingly new argument that may be worth looking into), talking to law professionals or legal academics, and so on.[3] At this stage, a systematic approach is neither required nor advised. Take your time to freely browse through everything the legal discipline has to offer and get intrigued by what you find, but make sure you force yourself to make a (first, provisional) topic choice at some point in the near future.

Regardless of how the topic you chose was singled out, we often find that the (first) topic novice researchers select is still too broad and/or not (yet) suitable for academic enquiry. The only way to remedy these flaws in a structured and efficient manner is by doing a systematic review of the literature on that (still provisional) topic. As we will try to show in the upcoming paragraphs, it is the systematic review of the literature that will allow you to translate your topic into an academic research question and even help you estimate how best to answer that question.

> Almost without exception, we can report that we have seen initial topics change dramatically after the performance of a literature review. You may, for instance, come across an interesting newspaper article on self-driving cars. That makes you wonder who would be liable for damages caused when a self-driving car is involved in a traffic accident. Some students would then instantly raise their research question (for instance, 'who is liable when damages are caused by a self-driving car?'). Without doing a literature review though, you do not know whether that question is still too broad to be answered comprehensively (*paragraph 2.4*), whether or not the question has been answered before and whether answering that question is significant for

---

2   Meeker's (1996) article provides several suggestions for how to find a research topic.

3   While it may be the case that by reading the literature you are first attracted to a particular topic, it may thus just as well be by coming across a legislative proposal or a new court decision. Some experienced researchers have even said they mainly find their research topics by going through primary sources, rather than secondary ones.

society and academic colleagues (*paragraph 2.5*), and whether that question is actually answerable at all (*paragraph 2.6*). By doing a literature review, you may, for instance, find that a lot has been written on liability and self-driving cars in general, but that there are interesting under-researched aspects such as the duty of care of the owner/driver of a self-driving car or the liability of a producer for not providing sufficient information on how to use a self-driving car. You might then rather focus your research question on one of those aspects (we will also address this point in *paragraph 3.5*).

2.3   Helping you to really understand your topic

Virtually every book on how to design and execute an academic research project has a strong emphasis on the importance of both having sufficient substantive knowledge of the research field *and* understanding the meta-physics of that field for doing academic research in that field (Oost, 1999, pp. 32-37).[4] Or, phrased differently: a viable research design can be constructed and executed only after the researcher possesses a "thorough knowledge of a field" (Hillway, 1969, p. 11; Hondius, 2007, p. 739). We do not know how to put this, except just to say it: the undergraduate and young postgraduate simply do not meet this criterion with respect to any area of the law (or doctrine) after having completed the courses taught at law school.[5]

The legal curriculum is generally organized in a way that allows students to obtain knowledge and understanding of the theoretical foundations and central issues and doctrines of the main fields of law (contract, tort, property, criminal, constitutional, administrative, and business law) instead of reaching the deeper knowledge necessary for conducting academic research in a particular field or on a particular doctrine. Moreover, course instructors typically prescribe textbooks that discuss a particular field of law and its doctrines in a broad sense and on the basis of the prevailing view held by the legal community. This implies that the law student is missing,

---

4   Therefore, it is hardly surprising that many doctoral students are only able to come up with their (more or less final) problem definition about halfway through their trajectory. Based on a regular trajectory, that is after one-and-a-half or two years of performing full-time research. A bachelor's or master's thesis trajectory, unfortunately, does not allow you to spend that much time on developing your problem definition.

5   That has made philosopher of science Bunge (1967) state that only experienced researchers are able to appreciate the scope and importance of a problem without severe time investment. Empirical studies undertaken in other academic disciplines have revealed that the lack of knowledge and experience of undergraduates is the most important factor for research failure (see Lagerwaard & Mul, 1982, p. 127; Verschuren & Doorewaard, 2010, pp. 9-10; Zuber-Skerritt & Knight, 1986, p. 89).

or only gets to see a first glimpse of, the in-depth discussions in which legal academics are engaged regarding nearly all legal doctrines.[6]

We have come across many examples of bachelor's and master's theses that ask the wrong questions (already answered, not answerable, or not legally relevant), contain substantive errors (incorrect interpretations of case law or legislation, sometimes even the use of obsolete rules), and show a lack of contextual understanding. To prevent this from happening, there is nothing for it but to make up for your backlog in knowledge by investing heavily in reading the literature that has appeared in relation to the topic you are interested in at the start of your research trajectory (Boote & Beile, 2005, p. 3; Hart, 2001, pp. 20-25; Hutchinson & Cuffe, 2003). After all, doing a literature review forces you to educate yourself with as much information as possible pertaining to the chosen topic (Denney & Tewksbury 2012, p. 219).

> The literature review will help you answer the following questions. How has a doctrine come to its current state and what really is that current state if we look at it in more detail? What *exactly* is the prevailing view with regard to the doctrine, but also: what alternatives and nuances on that prevailing view did other authors highlight? What links with other doctrines or fields have been established before? How about connections with theory and legal principles? Who are the authors that regularly publish in the field? What is the value and contribution of any one article in the light of other articles that address the same topic? How do all the studies on a topic fit together? And so on.[7]
>
> After reviewing the literature, you will at least have a much clearer picture of what it is you find interesting. It is not inconceivable (we came across many instances!) that what seemed to you to be a new, compelling topic may on second consideration be much less attractive than another angle you bumped into. Better to find that out before you invest a lot of time in your initial ideas!

2.4   Narrowing down your research topic

Doing a literature review at the initial stage of a research project may also help prevent you from having expectations that are far too great and from constructing a study design that is too broad and/or too ambitious to be carried out successfully. Law students, including doctoral students, usually start with an interest in a broad topic ('notice of default', 'product liability', 'contract law', 'human rights', 'sexual offences', and so on). Almost without exception, they initially seem to believe that their thesis (whether bachelor's, master's or doctoral) *must* be aimed at fully mapping *and* greatly improving (the law or the way in which the law is practiced with regard to) the topic they are interested in. When you take the entire body of legal

---

6   In this sense it is not that surprising that many of the research proposals for a bachelor's or master's thesis draw quite heavily from legal textbooks. Drawing from textbooks does not, however, enable you to achieve the know-how of the field necessary for drafting your literature review (see *paragraph 3.3*).

7   Questions we promise to get back to in the upcoming chapters.

literature, however, you will soon find out that there are almost no academic contributions[8] that endorse such high ambitions.[9] We believe early awareness of the fact that you should not be overambitious and that (a strict) delineation of your research topic is necessary means a great deal,[10] and studying the academic literature will definitely help you accomplish this.

> Reviewing the literature may assist the novice researcher in getting a sense of what is a researchable topic (narrow enough) within a broader research field and what is not (still too broad). For a bachelor's or master's thesis, we think you should generally be looking for a scope that is similar to or even tighter than that of the average journal article. The topic of a monography (including dissertations) – as a general rule, with exceptions – is probably too broad in this context.
>
> The topic Mak, for instance, addressed in her dissertation on '*Fundamental Rights in European Contract Law*' (2008) is an example of a topic that would not be feasible for a bachelor's or master's thesis. For you, as a novice researcher, to understand the whole field of fundamental rights, contract law, and how they may interact, would be too much to ask. You would be better off with a tighter question that can be answered by becoming familiar with more limited fields. You could, for instance, focus on the role that fundamental rights (might) play in the interpretation of contract terms[11] or on how these rights could influence questions of pre-contractual liability.
>
> If you are, for instance, interested in insurance policies, reviewing the literature will show you that the insurance policy as such is too broad to write about. Journal articles focus on questions on the level of protection that consumers enjoy against possibly unfair terms in insurance policies (see for instance Borselli's '*Unfair Terms in Insurance Contracts*', 2011) or the interpretation of terms in these contracts (see for instance Cohen and Quaintance's '*Role of Contra Proferentem in Interpretation of Insurance Contracts*', 1989). This teaches us that making a similar delineation is probably necessary to narrow down our broader topic to researchable proportions.

After having developed a sense of the kind of topic that is narrow enough to serve as the object of your research endeavor, the literature review may also reveal possible starting points for developing your research question. While we dig into this in more detail in *paragraph 2.5*, we would already like to state that you should be aware of the fact that there is a possibility that the review will indicate that there is no suitable aspect of your topic left for you to write your thesis on. In most cases

---

8   Neither from the hand of the most experienced law professors, nor the sometimes even more than a thousand-page dissertations.

9   We remark that we ourselves do not know of any projects where the research ambitions did not have to be adjusted downwards during the research trajectory (in the context of the doctoral thesis this was also remarked by Van Hoecke, 2010, pp. 37-38).

10   After all, the later in the trajectory this happens, the more work is done in vain.

11   Like Van Dam's '*Mensenrechten en uitleg van overeenkomsten*' (2011).

though, your review will provide you with one or more angles that you can explore in your thesis.[12]

2.5   Phrasing, embedding and justifying your research question

After having narrowed down your topic to a researchable size, you will be able to start the process of phrasing, embedding, and justifying your research question(s).[13] Here, the researcher needs to be guided by the standards academic research questions should meet.[14] According to Oost (1999, p. 69), who devoted his dissertation to developing such standards, a researcher should:

1. place a research question in its disciplinary context (*substantive embodiment*);
2. persuasively indicate why answering that question is significant for the academic discipline and society (*significance* and *originality*);
3. establish an exact definition of the concepts and elements that are tucked away in the question (*precision*);
4. clarify what needs to be done to gather the data/information necessary for answering the question (*methodical functionality*);
5. link up question, discipline, strategy, and answer (*consistency*);
6. enable a reader to check and judge everything you did in this respect (*exposition* – or, as we would put it, *accountability*).

According to Oost, these characteristics can only be achieved if the literature is reviewed systematically first (we will come back to this in *paragraph 6.4*).[15] We will explain why.

---

12 Sometimes, you may even run into a specific suggestion for further research. Wijkhuijs' dissertation on '*Administrative Response to Court Decisions*' (2007, pp. 174-175), for instance, contains such suggestions. As her study found that the impact of court decisions was not only influenced by the characteristics of the government agency but also by factors emanating from the field of law in which the government agency is operating, she suggests that further research may be done in this respect. In other instances you will have to identify the gaps, inconsistencies, significant controversies, and/or unanswered question within the literature yourself (see also *paragraph 6.3*).

13 As you will find out, during this process, you probably will refine both your question and the justification thereof a dozen times before you are happy with it.

14 It is only in exceptional cases (for instance when you join a project of a researcher or research group) that you may find yourself in a situation where you can start with a fully operational research question that meets all of the criteria we will discuss below.

15 In the words of Lovitts (2007, p. 44) "[t]he review provides context for and connects the question/problem to past and contemporary thought and research on the question/problem". See also Alvesson and Sandberg (2011, p. 252) who state that "spotting gaps in the literature is the chief way to identifying research questions".

Phrasing an original question

There is consensus in the academic community regarding the fact that academic research must in some way be original (Lovitts, 2007, pp. 31-33).[16] Consequently, the researcher must know *exactly* about the investigations performed by other scholars operating in a particular research field. What questions have been asked before? What approaches and methods were used for answering these questions? And what results were achieved? Only then, will the researcher be able to say with a degree of certainty which research areas have been overlooked or under-researched or which areas of research have not been examined previously using a particular theory or perspective (Alvesson & Sandberg, 2011, p. 249; Knopf, 2006, p. 127).[17] To be original, there is thus no other way than to systematically map the contributions of others to a particular field preliminary to making your own contribution. Doing so not only ensures that you do not reinvent the wheel (Bryman, 2008, p. 81), but may also inspire you to come up with your own, original approach or angle regarding a particular topic.[18]

> We remark, following Vranken (2014, pp. 50-51), that the researcher is not required to introduce a completely new idea, perspective or thought with the potential to change a doctrine or legal system. The novelty of the research question can be much more modest, but not, therefore, less useful. The researcher may, for instance, focus on adding a new aspect to the debate among legal scholars, pointing out a Supreme Court decision that may be interpreted differently than others have done before, considering the way in which district courts deal with open norms, or comparing a domestic doctrine with the situation abroad.[19] Also, we emphasize that being original does not imply that old questions may not be revisited or that settled debates may not be re-opened. What it does mean is that, if you wish to do so, you should credibly argue that your approach is original or that you are arguing against some of the long-standing views (see *paragraph 6.3*).

---

16   This is also the case for legal scholarship, as was recently confirmed by empirical research conducted by Snel (2017b).

17   Epstein and King (2002, pp. 56-57) provide an example of a publication (Sisk, Heise, and Morriss' *'Charting the Influences on the Judicial Mind: An Empirical Study of Judicial Reasoning'*, 1998) that claimed that "[t]hus far, public choice theory has had relatively little to say about judges' behavior in deciding cases", whereas there appeared to be many articles and books predating 1998 that had invoked public choice theory (or some variant thereof). Of course, making such misleading claims erodes the credibility of your enquiry.

18   Doing a literature review can, for instance, help you discover new linkages between different and formerly seemingly unrelated scholarly debates (see Aveyard, 2010, pp. 8-9).

19   The contribution of Siems (2008) can serve as an important source of inspiration for the researcher who is searching for an original angle.

Assessing your question's significance

The fact that you are adding something to the body of knowledge is, however, not enough to justify an academic research project. What is added must also be significant to the discipline. Legal scholars do not generally have any trouble explaining why what they do is relevant for *societal actors* or *society* as a whole (compare Epstein & King, 2002, p. 60); how the results of their research may help in making the life of lawyers, judges, legislators, insurers, and so on more easy, comfortable, efficient, effective, fairer or cheaper. In our experience, it is exactly that desire to improve something for someone that generally serves as the starting point of a student's thesis. Of course, it is great that your proposed project hooks up with societal questions and/or developments, but be aware that academic research must also carry *scientific significance* (compare Siems, 2008, pp. 147-148): it has to be significant for academic colleagues too.[20] This requires a clear picture of the issues that occupy academics in a certain field and thus a systematic review of the literature (Bryman, 2008, p. 81). Therefore, while the natural inclination to start a research project from a societal problem is understandable, it is only acceptable if combined with a systematic review of the academic literature.

Precise phrasing and embedment of your question

Systematically reviewing the literature also helps you *phrase* and *embed* your research question(s). After having read the literature published in a particular field, it will be much easier to use precise and correct language[21] when wording your question and to clarify the background against which your question can be understood. Moreover, the literature review is an excellent tool to make the way in which the significant contribution to the existing knowledge is sought transparent to the *reader*. By showing that earlier publications were consulted, by defining what has been done before and what has not, and by clarifying the knowledge that is significant to the field, the researcher is able to justify her question(s).[22] Indeed, without

---

20   Epstein and King (2002, pp. 56-58) provide three main reasons for the fact that addressing real-world problems is not enough: (*1*) finding a way to participate in the social enterprise of scholarship minimizes the chances that informed, and perhaps even uninformed, readers will question whether the researcher is up on the 'state of the art' in the particular area under analysis; (*2*) it decreases the chances of reinventing the wheel; and (*3*), it ensures that someone will be interested in the results.

21   See the editorial of the Journal of Criminal Justice Education, '*The Role of a Literature Review in Publication*' (1998), which states that "[l]iterature reviews are also an important method by which to introduce the reader to complex or new terminology or concepts that will be a part of the current discussion (…) When a review of concepts and terminology is included with the literature review, it also allows the author to direct the reader to additional sources of information where he or she may find a more detailed discussion".

22   From a somewhat different perspective, doing a literature review may also demonstrate that you have a firm understanding of the topic, providing credibility to you as an author and to your overall argument (Denney & Tewksbury, 2013, p. 219). See also

embedment and justification, a research question is nothing more than a hollow phrase.[23]

> "Use your review of the literature as a means of showing why your research questions are important. For example, if one of your arguments in arriving at your research questions is that, although a lot of research has been done on X (a general topic or area, such as the secularization process, female entrepreneurship, or employee absenteeism), little or no research has been done on X₁ (an aspect of X), the literature review is the point where you can justify this assertion. Alternatively, it might be that there are two competing positions with regard to X₁ and you are going to investigate which one provides a better understanding. In the literature review, you should outline the nature of the differences between the competing positions. The literature review, then, allows you to locate your own research within a tradition of research in an area" (Bryman, 2008, pp. 82-83).

2.6   Assessing your project's feasibility

The literature review may thus aid in finding, embedding and justifying a question that is worth answering. It should not be forgotten though, that it is equally important to consider, right from the start, whether that question can in fact be answered (within the available time frame) and, if that is the case, what the best way to do so is. Here too, the literature review can be of help in at least two different ways: by getting a sense of the approaches and methodological choices that have led to research success (publication) in the past and by knowing what kind of information (data) is available (and accessible) in the field in which the researcher is interested.[24]

> The literature review gives you an overview of the research methods and techniques used by other scholars operating in the field that interests you. Are the majority of the publications to be considered as doctrinal legal research (and are they, for instance, research that maps parliamentary documents or research aimed at discovering certain patterns and discrepancies in judicial opinions)? Is the research topic amenable to comparative analysis? And/or are there more or less convenient inter- or

---

Bryman (2008, p. 81) who states that "[a] competent review of the literature is at least in part a means of affirming your credibility as someone who is knowledgeable in your chosen area".

23   Often, we encounter situations in which our students come to us at the start of their research projects with provisional questions. Without any further information – indeed, without having performed a systematic literature review – it is almost always impossible to tell whether the question is suited to being answered within a thesis trajectory.

24   If you find an angle worth pursuing based on your literature review, that literature review alone will not often sufficiently enable you to assess whether your research question can be answered. In our view, you should therefore at least also conduct a pilot study that helps you find out whether pursuing that angle is feasible (see also Snel, 2017a).

multidisciplinary angles from which the research topic can be approached (and if so, what kind: law and economics, sociolegal, law and psychology, et cetera)? Besides that, the researcher may also – we think even more importantly – find inspiration in the way in which others operating in the field have actually used such methods. What exact steps did the author take when comparing the Dutch and German doctrine of duty of care in a contract law context and what can I learn by comparing it with the way in which the 'duty of care' is organized in the United Kingdom? How did the author make her selection of judicial opinions ruled by district courts and can I use similar criteria to make my own selection? And so on.

Ideally, at the start of her research project, the researcher will already have a clear picture of the information (data) that is both available and accessible and the information (data) that still has to be collected. What information is easily available and what is not, may follow from the works of others. If, for instance, you encounter a contribution that mentions a lot of district court decisions, this may be an indication that there are a lot of relevant judicial opinions ruled by district courts that you can work with. If there are regular references to international literature, this may mean that there is relevant literature to be found in international databases. And, if it turns out that other scholars have gained access to certain policy documents (from public prosecutors, for instance) or files (police files, for instance), this may encourage you to try to get similar access. In this way, you can make a more or less informed assessment of the feasibility of your research project which would not have been possible without doing the literature review.

2.7   So what is a systematic literature review and what is it not?

That pretty much brings us up to speed with the arguments in favor of doing a systematic literature review at the start of an academic research project. Now we know that the literature review is indispensable, we hope you already have a fairly clear idea about what we think a literature review should look like. Most importantly, we have seen that, according to our focus in this book, reviewing the literature at the start of your research trajectory is aimed at *finding* a research question, not *answering* one. We cannot stress this enough. A literature review *is not* a success if it answers the initial question you had in mind, it *is* a success if it proves that that answer is *not yet* sufficiently available.

Bruce's (1994) study of research students' early experiences of the dissertation literature review identified six qualitatively different ways in which the review process was experienced or understood by postgraduates:

1. a list comprising pertinent items representing the literature on the subject;
2. a process of identifying relevant information with a focus on finding or looking, which may involve going through sources to identify information;
3. an investigation of past and present writing or research on a subject, either active (critical/analytical) or passive (descriptive);
4. a vehicle for learning that leads to an increase in knowledge and understanding (sounding board through which the student can check ideas or test personal perceptions);

5. a process that helps the researcher identify a topic, support a methodology, provide a context or change research direction;
6. a written discussion of the literature focused on framing a written discourse about the literature which may be established as a component part of a thesis or other research report.

Based on the reasons we presented for doing a systematic literature review, we believe it to be all of these things at the same time.[25] Except, maybe, for the last bullet point, since – consistent with what is common practice in our discipline – we believe it is not per se necessary to present your literature review as an independent product at the beginning of your research trajectory. Sometimes your supervisor or course instructor *does* want you to do so before you start working on your research proposal. Mostly though, you will (often even implicitly) be expected to do all the work in the shadows of your actual research project. In such a case, you may of course write it down – we believe you can definitely benefit from doing so – but you may also choose to instantly convert and extend your literature review to a fully-fledged research proposal or research design. Thus, using your literature review to directly embed and justify the research question flowing from that review in a first paragraph or introductory chapter of your thesis.

Annoying as it may be, you will need to demonstrate (to the reader) that you undertook a comprehensive and systematic approach. Therefore, you should give a full account of your literature review *process*. You will thus need to document this process very clearly when you write your review. After all, if you do not document the process that was undertaken, the reader will be given the impression that it was not conducted (Aveyard, 2010, p. 149). When discussing the different steps of the literature review in **chapters 3 to 6**, we will pay specific attention to the question of how best to document what you have done.

2.8   Characteristics at different quality levels

Now that we know what a literature review is and why we need to do it, there is only one question left before we can move on to discussing the separate techniques of the systematic literature review: what constitutes a good literature review, and how can an excellent review be distinguished from a poor effort? Lovitts (2007, p. 54) carried out thorough empirical research (in ten different academic disciplines) on this question. As we cannot do more than she did, we would like to endorse her findings here (for an overview, see *table 2.1*). According to Lovitts (2007, p. 44):

> "[a]n *outstanding* review is important, relevant, analytical, and insightful. It reads like a good review article and educates the reader. Students who write outstanding literature reviews display a deep and sweeping grasp of the literature, often drawing on literatures from other fields. At the same time, they are selective, including only

---

25   Bruce himself recommends that students be encouraged to adopt the higher-level conceptions (3-6), because through these the other ways of experiencing the literature review (1-3) become more meaningful.

the most relevant and important works. They use the literature to show what is missing, why their project needs to be done, and how their research is going to advance the field. While critical, students who write outstanding literature reviews show empathy for and appreciation of others' work.

Very good literature reviews are critical and comprehensive. They help the reader understand the area under investigation. They tend to discuss everything that has been written on the topic, though may also miss some relevant parts of the literature.

Students who write *acceptable* literature reviews often take the literature they have read at face value and do not (or cannot) discriminate between good papers and bad ones. Their literature reviews are descriptive summaries, 'so-and-so and so-and-so said', that make obvious points.

Similarly, *unacceptable* reviews lack an organizing intelligence. Students who write them typically have not read enough. They fail to cite important papers, cite papers they have not read, and do not seem to understand their sources".

2.9　Summary and key points

In this chapter, our goal was to present the main reasons why it is crucial to do a literature review at the beginning of your research project. These reasons can be summarized in the following points:

1. a literature review will provide you with the necessary information about the field you are interested in so you can find a research question since you will learn about the central debates, remaining gaps and overlooked approaches;
2. the literature review will assist you in shaping your topic to a researchable size, so you avoid starting an overambitious project that you will not be able to conclude within the available time;
3. your research question will be embedded in a respectful body of knowledge, which will justify its significance to the field (*i.e.* how it adds to the academic debate) and provide the terminology you need to phrase your research questions (the main concepts you will use);
4. knowing the prior works, you will be able to estimate the time you will need to develop your own project, to elaborate on the methods you will employ, and to plan how to gather the data you will need.

In this chapter, we also wanted to demonstrate what a literature review is. In summary, a literature review is, all at the same time, a list of previous works, a process of getting acquainted with the discussions about your topic, an analytical and descriptive investigation, a vehicle for learning, a process for identifying a topic and a methodology, and a written discussion of the literature. An outstanding literature review shows that the reviewer fully understood the state of the art, is able to add to it by identifying missing points, and knows how to fill these gaps.

Table 2.1 **Characteristics of the literature review at different quality levels (Lovitts, 2007, p. 54)**

Quality levels

Outstanding	Very good	Acceptable	Unacceptable
– Comprehensive, thorough, complete, coherent, concise, and up to date – Shows critical and analytical thinking about the literature – Synthesizes the literature – Integrates literature from other fields – Displays understanding of the history and context of the problem – Identifies problems and limitations – Is selective – discriminates between important and unimportant works – Identifies and organizes analysis around themes or conceptual categories – Adds own insights – Uses the literature to build an argument and advance the field – Makes reader look at the literature differently	– Comprehensive but not exhaustive – Provides a thoughtful, accurate critique of the literature – Shows understanding of and command over the most relevant literature – Selects literature wisely and judiciously – Sets the problem in context – Uses literature to build a case for the research	– Provides adequate coverage of the literature – Demonstrates that student has read and understood the literature – Lacks critical analysis and synthesis – Is not selective, does not distinguish between more- and less-relevant works – Misses some important works – Cites some works that are not relevant – Is an undifferentiated list, "This person said this, this person said that" – Does not put problem in context	– Missing, inadequate, or incomplete – Has not read enough and does not cite enough sources – Misinterprets or does not understand the literature – Misses, omits, or ignores important studies, whole areas of literature of people who have done the same thing – Cites sources student has not read or where she has only read the abstract – Cites articles that are out of date – Does not provide a context for the research

25

3 Preparing for your literature review

3.1 Introduction

In the previous chapter we learned that a literature review is a means of (*1*) getting acquainted with your research topic, (*2*) narrowing down the (broader) topic you started with to researchable proportions, (*3*) phrasing, embedding and justifying a research question, and (*4*) assessing your project's feasibility. Now we know the *why*, it is time to look at the *how*. In the upcoming chapters, we will discuss the different steps we believe you should take to give your research project the best possible start.

After you chose your (provisional, see *paragraph 2.2*) topic, the first thing we recommend is to get a sense of the information you will need to include in or exclude from your review. This is a vital step. With respect to virtually any topic you will encounter a large variety of material that somehow seems related to your project and you simply cannot include all of it. Instead of jumping in an endless sea of information (with a real chance of drowning), you should think of a strategy that prevents you from spending your precious time on collecting and processing the wrong information. Part of that strategy should at least be to make sure your topic is delineated enough (*paragraph 3.5*) and that you have an idea about how wide you are going to cast your net (*paragraph 3.6*).

Before you come to that stage, however, it is important for you to be able to recognize the different types of information that may or may not be relevant to your review. Therefore, we will provide a brief overview of the information you are likely to encounter and some *general* information on its potential for your literature review.[1] Firstly, we will distinguish between primary and secondary materials (*paragraph 3.2*). Secondly, we will talk you through the different types of secondary materials (*paragraph 3.3*). And finally, we will present the most common research approaches that legal scholars adopt (*paragraph 3.4*). Issues related to reviewing and critiquing the different materials you may come across will be discussed in **chapter 5**. Information about the process of attaching cogency to these materials is provided in **chapter 6**.

---

1 We will be brief here, as others have dealt with this in more detail before, see for instance Finch and Fafinski (2015), Tjaden (2010), and Hanson (2016).

3.2 Primary versus secondary sources

Legal sources are usually divided into primary and secondary materials. A *primary source* can be defined as a statement of the law itself from a governmental entity, such as a court, the legislature, or an executive agency. The most important examples of primary sources are court decisions of national and international courts, opinions of other arbitrators, regulations enacted by competent national and regional (*e.g.* European, African, Asian) institutes that are recognized by the law itself, explanatory memoranda or other official commentaries provided by the enacting institution(s), policy, soft law, self-regulation, and contracts (Cohen & Olson, 2007, pp. 6-8). *Secondary sources* are the materials that discuss, explain, interpret, analyze, or comment on one or more primary sources and/or the doctrine[2] they together form. Examples are publications in law reviews, books, and case notes (see *paragraph 3.3* for a more elaborate overview).

As its name suggests, the literature review focuses on *secondary* sources. However logical that may sound, we cannot emphasize this enough. In exercises where students were asked to write a literature review, we often find them starting by spending several pages describing the legislation and case law related to their topic. Apparently, there is a deep-seated tendency amongst law students – perhaps because of the fact that legal education is mainly focused on solving cases by reference to legislation and case law – to start by using primary materials. That is problematic in the context of academic research, as merely describing the current state of the law does not, in itself, result in a new, unanswered research question. After all, for that the researcher will need to find out what inquiries other *legal scholars* have already conducted in relation to these primary materials.

> To be blunt, a literature review should thus not, for example, start like this: 'The nemo tenetur principle is based on article 6 of the ECHR. In its case law, the ECtHR established a right for anyone charged with a criminal offence (...) to remain silent and not to incriminate himself' and the subsequent discussion of the considerations of the ECtHR in Funke,[3] Saunders,[4] and J.B. versus Switzerland.[5] Rather, it should, for instance, commence something like this: 'The German literature on the application of the nemo tenetur principle in the area of tax law reveals that the principle is not interpreted consistently. Several authors argue that the *Bun-*

---

2   A doctrine is best described as an intellectual construct, framework, set of rules, or system of logically coherent, non-contradictory assertions, ideas and concepts that relate to a particular legal (sub)system (Tiller & Cross, 2006, p. 517). Doctrines can take many different forms; they may be 'very fact-dependent or of sweeping breadth'. Some doctrines refer to concrete legal provisions, others to more fundamental legal principles. Examples are the doctrines of 'good faith', 'breach of contract', 'duty of care' (contract law), and 'culpa' (or criminal negligence), 'conditional intent', 'minimum of evidence' (criminal law).

3   ECHR 25 February 1993, Application no. 10828/84 (*Funke v. France*).

4   ECHR 17 December 1997, Application no. 19187/91 (*Saunders v. United Kingdom*).

5   ECHR 3 May 2000, Application no. 311827/96 (*J.B. v. Switzerland*).

desverfassungsgericht should reconsider its earlier opinion on the scope of the nemo tenetur principle. The reasons they provide for this are (…)'.

Do not be mistaken here. Of course, it is important that, from the beginning of your project, you also collect, read, interpret, and analyze primary sources on the area that you are interested in. It will help you to get acquainted with your topic and to understand the secondary sources you will need to use for the construction of your literature review. At the stage of doing a literature review, however, you should refrain from writing too much about the primary sources themselves. Save it for later, when you know more precisely what your research project is going to be about (*e.g.* when you have identified your research question). Perhaps – and this is far from unusual – you then will find that describing the (complete) current state of the law relating to your topic is superfluous. For instance, because others have done it before and referring to their contributions suffices or because you end up with an interdisciplinary research question that does not require you to write about the primary legal sources on your topic at all.

3.3   Types of sources you are likely to encounter

Secondary sources come in many different shapes and sizes. We will distinguish four main categories: (*1*) contributions in law reviews or journals, (*2*) books, (*3*) reflections on the law in response to specific legal disputes, and (*4*) publicly accessible working papers, reports, blogs and commentaries posted online.

Contribution in law reviews or journals

Most of what legal scholars produce can be found in national and international law journals. Be aware, though, that what is published in law journals has no single, uniform format. It ranges from 'academic' (increasing the body of knowledge) to 'professional' publications (merely disseminating knowledge among practitioners and students); from lengthy pieces to short opinions, essays or book reviews. Generally, the more deliberate academic pieces are what you want to build on when you are doing your literature review. We use 'generally', because it cannot be ruled out that the shorter, opinion-forming pieces or contributions aimed at practitioners contain ideas or insights that could enrich your literature review (see also *paragraph 5.3*). Therefore, while you may – must even – focus on academic works, keep an eye open for all kinds of other contributions you may find in the law journals.

We have to remark, though, that it is not always easy to instantly classify a particular publication as 'academic' or 'professional'. Not all law journals make that distinction or, if they do,[6] rigorously enforce it.[7]

A somewhat separate category of contributions that can be found in some law journals are chronicles and annual collections of papers, in which the records and reports of a learned field are compiled (Stolker, 2014, p. 257). While they generally do not contain new insights, they may point the researcher to materials that she *can* use for the construction of her literature review.

Books

Apart from being published in law journals, a substantial proportion of legal scholarship is published in books.[8] With respect to nearly all doctrines, fields and sub-fields of the law, there are scholarly monographs (including PhD dissertations), textbooks, casebooks and commentaries. Like contributions in law journals, these books also vary in the public they address (academics, students, professionals), scope, length and depth. Monographs (including dissertations) are often the result of a long-lasting research project with a relatively circumscribed focus. They generally intend to cover everything that has happened on the topic they address. That means that they not only contain a high-density of sources that you can scoop up, but also often reveal interesting angles – sometimes even explicated suggestions – for further research. That turns monographs into the most important category of books for your literature review.

Textbooks differ from monographs in the sense that they are usually written for educational purposes. They often represent the standard form of expression of particular areas of law, largely omitting the underlying debates, alternative views, and non-legal contextual information.[9] While that makes textbooks less useful for drafting your literature review (compare Denney & Tewksbury, 2013, pp. 227-228; Tjong Tjin Tai, 2017, p. 24; Van Dijck, 2016, p. 11), this does not mean that they may or should be completely neglected. On the contrary, consulting textbooks may be helpful for determining the prevailing view of a particular legal doctrine and/or to get an overview of the disciplinary context of your topic.[10]

---

6   The *Nederlands Juristenblad*, for example, does. It has different sections for scientific articles, lessons for practice, essays, opinion pieces, and brief commentaries, see <http://njb.nl/auteursaanwijzingen>. The Oxford Journal of Legal Studies, for example, claims it only publishes original (academic) contributions and no other pieces, see <https://academic.oup.com/ojls/pages/General_Instructions>.

7   See also van Gestel and Lienhard's '*The Advantage of Lagging Behind*' (forthcoming).

8   Stolker (2014, p. 248) noted that legal scholarship has a strong tradition in book publishing. He however adds: "although I do not want to go as far as the university librarian (…) who considered books nowadays as 'mainly good for acoustics', I expect journal publications to become the most important medium of legal scholarship in our time".

9   There are, however, exceptions, such as the Dutch *Asser Series*.

10   Your topic may be discussed among various other topics that the author of a textbook has clustered for a reason.

Legal encyclopedias and casebooks, finally, can be of use for your research project – as they may redirect you to relevant primary materials – but generally not for your literature review.[11] They are usually written in propositional style, which means that they comprise a series of statements or propositions about the law, where every statement is supported by primary sources. They do not attempt to look at the history of the law or examine its social context. They will not express an opinion about the law. Viewed together, this leads us to believe that going through these materials will not be of much help when you are trying to phrase and embed an academic research question.

Reflections on the law in response to specific legal disputes

So-called case notes are specific to the legal discipline. Case law regularly sparks a response from legal scholars and law professionals that may result in a case note which may or may not be published. Apart from that, in some instances, specific legal disputes that are submitted to the court (mainly higher courts, such as the European Court of Justice and the Dutch Supreme Court) elicit an opinion (*conclusion*) of an Attorney General before being decided. What case notes and conclusions have in common is that they may range from very brief or case-specific comments to sometimes quite lengthy analytical and comparative reflections that add several new insights to the existing body of knowledge. The latter type should not – if available on your topic – be omitted from your review.

> There are several areas (depending on which jurisdiction you are looking into though) where you will have to rely largely on case notes, since there is a lack of academic journal articles and reflective books. In the Netherlands, for instance, this may be the case when you are writing on how banks deal with security rights (pledge and mortgage).

Working papers, reports, blogs and commentaries posted online

A final group of secondary sources is sometimes referred to as 'grey literature'. Rucinski (2015) has explored the history, definitions, and characteristics of grey literature. He provides an overview of the types of grey legal information resources: archives, blogs,[12] bulletins, business records, conference materials, correspondence, e-mails, logs, memoranda, newsletters, reports, surveys, websites, working papers (for instance those posted on *ssrn.com* or personal websites of scholars and institutes), and so on. In our experience, law students tend to rely quite heavily on this

---

11   Meeker (1996, p. 922) however, emphasizes that casebooks tend to emphasize unsettled points of law and can therefore be helpful in determining a researchable area.

12   According to Stolker (2014, p. 258), blogs "may become a great tool for international scholarly debate, as well as for the debate within society at large". In itself though, he adds – and we agree – "a blog or column can never be a formal product of scholarly research". Examples of well-known blogs in legal scholarship are the Scotusblog (<www.scotusblog.com>), the European Law Blog (<http://europeanlawblog.eu>) and the Dutch *cassatieblog* (<https://cassatieblog.nl/>).

category of sources, perhaps because they are easily accessible through Google. We, however, think that as a rule – and we remind you that all rules have exceptions – those sources are less valuable for your literature review than academic journal articles and books (compare Tjong Tjin Tai, 2017, p. 24; Van Dijck, 2016, p. 8) and should therefore be used sparingly and with caution (Denney & Tewksbury, 2013, p. 228). Generally, thus, we recommend that you do not spend too much time on collecting and processing these sources, but rather perform a quick scan to make sure you do not miss the gems amongst them.

> Exceptions to this rule can be particular governmental publications (for instance evaluations of certain programs operated by government agencies and up to date statistics) or certain well-developed working papers published on *ssrn.com*. If, for example, your research topic is on budget cuts to juvenile substance abuse programs and anecdotal evidence is needed to support a theme found in the research, then a newspaper or magazine might also be an excellent source for making this point.

3.4 Types of research you are likely to encounter

Legal scholars are certainly not just involved in only one type of research. As Epstein and King (2002, p. 2) stated, "[t]he law reviews are replete with articles ranging from the normative to the descriptive, from narrow doctrinal analyses to large-sample-size (large-*n*) statistical investigations. Some studies advocate legal reform; others intend solely to add to the store of academic knowledge". In fact, there can be as many purposes for legal enquiries as there are legal scholars or objects of enquiry. All we can do here is present a simple typology that may help you go through your secondary sources. Therefore, we will stick with the more common distinction between doctrinal research, comparative law, legal history, jurisprudence, empirical legal studies, and 'law and' approaches (compare Rubin, 2001, p. 8677; Smits, 2015, p. 7). Please be aware, though, that two or more of these research approaches are sometimes – often, perhaps – combined in a single publication (Van Gestel & Micklitz, 2014, pp. 309-310).

Doctrinal legal research

Traditionally, the majority of enquiries undertaken by legal scholars can be typified as doctrinal legal research (Bartie, 2010; Stürner, 2012, p. 11; Vranken, 2014, p. 15). While (slightly) different views exist, we understand doctrinal legal research to be the type of research that is concerned with the study of positive law – as enshrined in primary sources – and future law (compare McCrudden, 2006, p. 634). In doctrinal legal research, positive law and its sources are studied from the assumption that the law represents a more or less coherent and consistent system, or – better formulated – a more or less coherent whole of different systems that exist on different levels of abstraction (compare Vranken, 2014, p. 64).[13]

The various aims pursued by doctrinal legal research stem from exactly this assumption. Without the pretense of being complete, we mention: (*a*) describing

---

13   For instance private law, contract law, and consumer law.

or disclosing (an aspect of) a system of positive law, (*b*) clarifying, explaining, or critically reflecting on possible imperfections, ambiguities and inconsistencies of (a part of) a legal system, (*c*) the placing of new societal changes or developments in national, European or international case law and legislation into the (domestic) legal system, (*d*) predicting future developments on the basis of the existing legal system, and (*e*) promoting the coherence and consistency of the system and establishing, refining, and improving the law based on criteria derived from the legal system itself (based on Kestemont, 2016, pp. 118-120; Rubin, 1997, p. 111; Scordato, 2008, p. 368; Stürner, 2012, p. 11).[14]

Comparative law

Apart from doctrinal legal research, legal scholars also study the relationship between legal systems (common and civil law, or Italian and French law), between the rules of more than one system,[15] between inter- or supranational regulations,[16] and between inter- or supranational law *and* domestic law.[17] These comparative law projects are pursued with several different aims in mind (Dannemann, 2006, pp. 402-406; Van Hoecke, 2015, pp. 2-3). A first major branch of comparative legal scholarship focuses on the unification or harmonization of legal rules within various legal systems. Secondly, comparative law enquiries are frequently carried out as part of an effort to contribute to one's own legal system: *e.g.* to improve a legal rule or institution that has been suspected or recognized as a source of problems,[18] but also just to achieve a better understanding of domestic law. Finally, comparative law may be used as an instrument of learning and knowledge in a more general way (information on the law elsewhere and a better understanding thereof) or as an instrument of evolutionary and taxonomic science (common evolutions, diachronic changes, legal families, et cetera).

Legal history

Legal scholars also regularly have recourse to history. A core aim of legal history is to provide insight into the mechanisms and dynamics of legal change (Handler, 2013, p. 95). Lesaffer (2011) distinguished three different ways of doing so. Firstly,

---

14 Quintessential doctrinal legal questions are the following: 'When does a duty under public law exist to effectively enforce public law?', 'Under what conditions is a governmental agency civilly liable for damages caused by insufficient monitoring and enforcement performance?', and 'What is the meaning of the lex-certa principle for Dutch criminal law, what should its meaning be and what requirements flow from this principle for the legislature when enacting criminal law provisions?'

15 'In the Netherlands, Germany and United Kingdom, which factors influence the determination of criminal liability of joint principals?'

16 For instance Battjes' *'European Asylum Law and International Law'* (2006).

17 For instance Reydams' *'Universal Jurisdiction. International and Municipal Legal Perspectives'* (2004).

18 Legislature, courts, and academics often take an interest in how other legal systems solve the problem for which a solution is sought.

there is the study of *history in law*.[19] This is the type of scholarship where legal scholars refer to the past in order to argue for the existence of a certain rule or a particular interpretation of that rule. The primary concern of this type of scholarship is not with history itself, but with what can be gained from it: an authoritative argument for the existence or interpretation of the rule. Secondly, there is *law in history*.[20] This refers to the study of law within its social, economic, cultural, and political context. The object of the study is the mutual interaction between law and society at a certain time and place in history. The central question here is what the law was and how it functioned in society at that time and place. Thirdly, there is *history of law*. This type of legal historical literature holds a middle position in the continuum between the former two. Its purpose is also to understand what the law was at a certain time and place in history, but now from a strictly legal perspective. It only differs from the doctrinal study of contemporary law in that it concerns the law from the past. The object of the study may either be the legal system as a whole, or just a particular branch, institution, principle, rule, or concept.

Jurisprudence

Legal scholars also engage in a type of scholarship usually called 'legal theory' or 'jurisprudence'.[21] Jurisprudence is a multifaceted phenomenon; the works presented under the label jurisprudence are very much a mixed bag (Wahlgren, 2005, p. 506). To keep it somewhat simple, we would say that scholarship that can be classified as jurisprudence focuses on a wide range of fundamental questions, such as the nature, sources, purposes and legitimacy of the law or legal systems, and the existence or non-existence of universal normative principles (Posner, 1993, p. xi; Rubin, 2001, pp. 8677-8678; Smith, 1998, pp. 3-4). Examples of this type of scholarship are the well-known works of authors like *Dworkin, Hart, Kelsen, Rawls, Von Savigny, Bentham, Luhmann* and many others, including all those they inspired to further expand or criticize their ideas. The most important difference between jurisprudence and doctrinal legal research is that the latter is said to be performed based on contemporary consensus regarding the answers given by scholars operating in the field of jurisprudence (Bodig, 2011, p. 7; Westerman, 2011, p. 91).

Empirical legal studies

Enquiries that can be referred to as 'empirical legal studies' are relatively new to legal scholarship. While the exact contours of this type of scholarship and its relationship to other forms of legal scholarship are still taking shape, we will use the

---

19   This approach is referred to as 'internal history' as well (see Handler, 2013, p. 86; Ibbetson, 2003, pp. 33-34). An example is Baker's, 'An Introduction to English Legal History' (2002).

20   This approach is also referred to as 'external history' (see Handler, 2013, p. 86).

21   The term 'legal theory' is also used in a broader sense, sometimes also including the 'law and' approaches that are discussed hereafter (see for instance Vilaça, 2015, pp. 792-801).

description of the different types of empirical legal scholarship that Korobkin (2002, pp. 1037-1045) provided to give you a basic idea about what it entails. Korobkin's typology is based on (*1*) the empirical data that is being relied on and (*2*) the descriptive or normative purposes of the research endeavor.

Firstly, there are studies that attempt to systematically analyze all judicial opinions relating to a particular topic over a certain period of time, for instance in order to draw conclusions (whether or not by using statistical analysis) about what objective factors drive court determinations of whether or not the promisor is liable to the promissee.[22] Secondly, there are studies that observe the actual behavior of legal actors, for instance by describing contracting patterns and norms generally followed by a particular type or group of contracting parties, by interviewing contract decision makers or by examining a large number of contracts.[23] Thirdly, empirical legal studies can be shaped as experimental studies, for instance designed in a way that allows the researcher to see how legal actors react to different legal scenarios.[24] And fourthly, there are empirical legal studies that rely on surveys of non-experts about their perceptions of what, for instance, contract law does and/or should require of contracting parties.[25]

Considering the purposes of the enquiry (the uses to which the data are put) rather than the source of the empirical data itself, a slightly different distinction can be made. Firstly, empirical data can be used to understand the contours of a doctrine (positive doctrinal analysis). Be aware that empirically driven positive analysis, whether based on qualitative assessments of large numbers of cases or quantitative assessments, has a different goal than what we called doctrinal legal research above, namely to look beyond judges' professed reasoning to identify what objectively identifiable factors actually drive case outcomes. Secondly, empirical data can be used to understand how doctrine affects the behavior of legal actors. And thirdly, empirical data can also be used to support proposed doctrinal shifts, or, in other words, to provide support for the author's normative argument for doctrinal change or reinforcement.

Interdisciplinary research – 'law and' approaches

In common parlance, the concept of interdisciplinarity is often used as a rather broad category encompassing all kinds of research in which two or more disciplines – law and politics, anthropology, race, economics, psychology, development, aes-

---

22 An example is Farber & Matheson's '*Beyond Promissory Estoppel: Contract Law and the "Invisible Handshake"*' (1985). These types of studies are different from doctrinal legal scholarship in the sense that "they attempt to use objective facts found in judicial opinions as data points in their analysis, rather than examining the internal logic or reasoning of opinions" (Korobkin, 2002, p. 1040).

23 For example, Macauly's '*Non-Contractual Relations in Business: A Preliminary Study*' (1963) and Cowan & Billaud's '*Between learning and schooling: the politics of human rights monitoring at the Universal Periodic Review*' (2015).

24 An example is Schwab's '*A Coasean Experiment on Contract Presumptions*' (1988).

25 For example, Kim's '*Bargaining with Imperfect Information: A Study of Worker Perceptions of Legal Protection in an At-Will World*' (1997).

thetics, deconstruction, music, literature, postmodern studies, ethics, and so on – are brought together (Taekema & Van Klink, 2011, p. 6). While some have contested the idea of the so-called 'law and' approaches as a distinct category of legal scholarship – some put them under the heading of legal theory (Vilaça, 2015, pp. 782-801), others under the heading of empirical legal studies (or the other way around) – we will address these approaches separately.

As we cannot discuss all the distinct interdisciplinary approaches that exist in detail, let us briefly look at two of the most common types. The first one is the discipline of law and economics. This combinatory study proposes a twofold program: (1) a re-description of existing legal rules according to economic concepts and theories such as incentives, transaction costs, and rational-choice theory; and (2) the evaluation of existing legal rules from an efficiency point of view, reducing justice and other substantive goals of positive law to economic efficiency (Posner, 2010). The second is the scholarship that can be categorized as law and humanities. Often, law and humanities scholarship is defined and defended on the basis of its contribution to the development of an ethically richer and more sensitive legal consciousness – *i.e.* one that listens to 'the other' and is conducive to the transformation of existing practices and institutions. Thus, law and humanities writings seek to educate a generation of lawyers to be better people and more in tune with the demands of justice (Vilaça, 2015, p. 798).

More generally, Taekema and Van Klink (2011) provided a typology of interdisciplinary research on a scale from a monodisciplinary towards a fully integrated interdisciplinary perspective. The first type of legal research that moves beyond the discipline of law is research that uses other disciplines heuristically. In such research, the legal discipline provides the problem definition, but the researcher also looks for useful material or ideas in another discipline. The second type uses other disciplines as auxiliary disciplines. The legal researcher defines a problem, which she cannot solve with legal methods only, so there is a need for input from another discipline.[26] The third type of research is comparative, treating two disciplines as equally important perspectives.[27] Perspectivist research then, switches between two disciplines, using the concepts and methods of each.[28] Finally, there is fully integrated interdisciplinary research. In this case, the research process itself contains elements from both disciplines and the researcher welds together the con-

---

26 Often there will be a reason for that problem, external to the legal framework, which is perceived as demanding a legal response. In this type of research, material derived from the other discipline serves as a necessary contribution to the legal arguments.

27 In this form of multidisciplinary research, each of the disciplines provides a definition of the central problem. There is no dominant perspective, and the core of such research is a comparative study of the two disciplines, in which the confrontation with the other discipline yields new insights for both.

28 The conclusions will also be perspectivist: there is not a coherent single answer, but a necessary co-existence of two disciplines. Neither discipline can provide the whole answer, nor can the disciplines give up their own framework.

cepts and methods from each or applies a more general methodological approach to both.[29]

3.5   Delineating your topic before starting your literature review

Now that we know we should focus our literature review on secondary sources (*paragraph 3.2*) and have obtained a pretty clear idea about what type of secondary sources exist (*paragraph 3.3*) and the research approaches they may represent (*paragraph 3.4*), we will take a closer look at the strategy we think you should develop in order to be able to efficiently execute your literature review. In **chapter 2,** we saw that doing a literature review is necessary for narrowing down the broader topic you started with to an academic research question that is not only worth answering but also answerable. That does not, however, mean that the process of delineation only commences with the start of your literature review (see *figure 3.1*). Some initial research interests are so broad ('human rights', 'tax evasion') that there is such an overwhelming number of secondary sources (and primary too, of course) the researcher can draw from, that making any sense of the complete body of literature related to such a topic is simply impossible.[30] Therefore, we believe the first thing you should do – *before* you start your literature review – is make sure that your topic has a tight focus.

Figure 3.1   Stages of narrowing down your topic

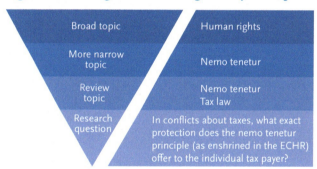

---

29   Application of the general methods of hermeneutics to both law and philosophy might serve as an example of the latter. An example of the integration of elements from two disciplines may be found in White's '*Law and Literature: No Manifesto*' (1988). He brings together concepts and methods from the legal and the literary perspective to create a new approach to both legal and literary texts.

30   A project often starts with a broad research topic or area of interest. At undergraduate level, that topic or area is often defined by your instructors. It may be broad (privacy and criminal law, product liability risk) or more narrow. In all instances though, you will have to find a more specific angle to bring your topic to researchable proportions.

Your topic should be focused, but not too narrow. A good topic to start your literature review with is one that is clear and specific. The remit of it should be small, but not so small that there is no identifiable literature to review (compare Aveyard, 2010, pp. 31-32). Tjong Tjin Tai (2017, pp. 43-45) refers to the process of focusing your topic as the 'orientation cycle' (as opposed to a 'main cycle' and 'checking' cycle, which are basically covered in **chapter 4**) and warns that "a common mistake in student papers is that the student stops with the orientation cycle and writes an essay on the basis of his results" but that "[t]his is not scientific research and the result is not (…) valid".

There is no official guide that explains how to go about this phase of your research project. We would argue that it is fair to say that, as a rule, focusing on a complete legal field (contract law, human rights) or even all aspects of a quite broad doctrine (tort of negligence) is generally far too extensive and complex to be dealt with comprehensively. Therefore, if you are still focused on a complete legal field or broad doctrine, we advise that you spend a certain (but limited!) amount of time to freely (so, no systematic searching and no tracking of what you are doing required here) go through any materials you come across in order to find a more specific angle that interests you (compare Aveyard, 2010, p. 27; Tjong Tjin Tai, 2017, p. 27). What might also help is to think about what should be *excluded* from your topic. The choices you make in this respect may be content-related (*e.g.* focusing on just one of the many human rights, for instance the nemo tenetur principle, leaving out the rest), systematic (*e.g.* the influence of human rights in the area of *private law*, not other legal areas; or only focus on French law), or pragmatic (*e.g.* excluding 'law and' approaches or electronic sources).

We suggest – we recognize that this is somewhat arbitrary though – that you perform a litmus test here. If you enter your (exact) topic in the open search field of one of the major legal databases in your jurisdiction (filtering on secondary sources only) and that gives you, say, 500 or more results, your topic is probably still too broad to make it the object of your literature review. Further delineation is then recommended.[31]

If we search for 'human rights' in only the Dutch database Legal Intelligence, we find over 200,000 hits, of which over 43,000 are categorized by the database as 'literature'. That is too many to map systematically, especially when we realize – as we discuss in **chapter 4** – that we cannot rely on just one database and that we will have to use additional search techniques (such as 'snowballing') as well. When we start reading freely with the aim of discovering a more specific angle in the field of human rights, we come across the *nemo tenetur*-principle. As this principle triggers an interest in us, we then repeat the same litmus test. We now find 2026 results, of which 1100 are categorized as literature. Still too many. When continuing our reading, we encounter an interesting article about the *nemo tenetur*-principle in a tax law

---

31   While 500 may sound excessive, from our experience, further filtering (leaving out random results that always pop up for some reason, results that seem irrelevant by only looking at the title or sources that are not secondary sources when looked at closely) will leave you with a list that is possible to go through.

journal. That provokes further demarcation of our topic to the applicability of the *nemo tenetur*-principle in the field of tax law. Again, repeating our litmus test, we get 620 hits, of which a little less than 500 are categorized as literature. That makes us more confident about the fact that we might now have found an angle that allows us to systematically map what has been written about it. Of course, later on, our angle might still prove to be too sweeping so that we have to delineate further, but at least we have a feasible topic for *starting* our literature review. That is, we remind you again, very different from the delineation necessary for *formulating your research question*.

After you have delineated your topic, it might be helpful to formulate a *review* – not a *research* – objective or question, as that will help focus the process that follows (Aveyard, 2010, p. 36; Bryman, 2008, p. 103). Think about questions like: 'what are the controversial and uncontroversial points among authors regarding the admissibility requirements of a given appeal?', 'what are the legal principles and theories mentioned by the authors with respect to the political role of supreme court justices?', and 'what does academic literature identify as the major discussions around the extraterritorial application of law?'. While we recommend establishing a *review* question, we would at the same time like to emphasize that doing so should not prevent you from letting yourself be surprised by the literature you come across. The *review* question should be used as guidance and should not keep you from finding something you were not expecting. In any circumstance, of course, you will be able to revise and refine your *review* objective or question (broadening it or narrowing it down) later on in the process of reviewing the literature (Aveyard, 2010, p. 39; Hutchinson & Cuffe, 2003).

To help you find your way, we will provide a few examples from our own experience of how broader topics were transformed into workable objects of a systematic literature review. An example of this is the research one of us supervised that started with the topic of 'the interplay between privacy and investigative powers when criminal offences are committed'. Eventually, after a period of brainstorming, the topic the literature review was written on was 'under what circumstances is the way in which investigating authorities make use of automated tracking systems when going through social media, still compliant with article 8 of the European Convention of Human Rights'. Another student started her thesis trajectory with an interest in self-driving cars. There is an abundance of (international) material related to the phenomenon, so that it was not suitable for performing a systematic literature review. Further orientation eventually resulted in the delineation (even a slightly shift) of her topic to 'liability of producers of products for providing insufficient or inadequate information to the users of the product'. Finally, we mention a project that started with the idea of looking at *ex officio* reviews of legal provisions. Before starting the literature review, the project had been delineated to '*ex officio* reviews of legal provision that protect consumers' rights when engaged in online purchasing'.

3.6   How wide should you cast your net?

Once you have delineated your topic, there is one more thing you need to consider before you can start your systematic search for relevant literature sources. That is the – difficult – question of how wide you should cast your net. Unfortunately, we believe that this question cannot be answered in general terms. How it should be answered depends on many different factors, among which, at least, the exact circumstances under which a research project is started (what knowledge the researcher already has about the topic, for instance) and the initial topic (for instance, is it about a doctrine that is influenced by European or international law?). What we can do, however, is show – by presenting several examples – how the determination of how wide to cast your net could take shape in hypothetical research projects.

Prior to that, some remarks can be made. As a general rule, your literature review should *focus* on those studies pertinent to the *specific* issue you plan to address (studies that match the topic of the third layer of the inverted pyramid, see *figure 3.1*). For example, if you delineated your topic to the 'liability of producers of products for providing insufficient or inadequate information to the users of the product', then make your search center on the literature others have written about *exactly* this. Do not spend much time on collecting and processing information on issues that you placed out of the scope of your literature review (layers one and two of the inverted pyramid, see *figure 3.1*).

Be aware, though, that every topic *is* part of a broader context (on a doctrinal, international and regional, societal and interdisciplinary level). As we saw in *paragraph 2.8*, an outstanding literature review also displays understanding of the context of a problem. You are, therefore, required to include *some* contextual material. As a minimum, if there is international or regional (like European) law that is relevant to the (part of the) domestic doctrine you are interested in, your literature review must include – if available – that international or European debate on the issues you plan to address (Snel, 2016, pp. 48-49; Vranken, 2014, pp. 23-34). To what extent you should also look for material that relates to the doctrinal context (the broader system the doctrine you are focusing on is part of and/or other neighboring doctrines), is harder to determine. We would say that while such materials cannot be omitted completely, you should not strive for full coverage here, as that will eventually drag you away from what is pertinent to your study. Finally, we believe that, in principle, material that is produced in other disciplines (economics, sociology, psychology, and so on) is best left aside.[32] As you are a *legal* scholar (not an economist, sociologist or psychologist) who is adding to the *legal* scholarly

---

32 That does not mean that such materials cannot be used for *answering* a research question. Suppose you get the impression that psychological knowledge about warnings might be of interest for a doctrine in tort law. The literature review should be aimed at finding out whether others think so too and/or whether other legal scholars have used psychological insights before and what they found by doing so. In the literature review, we do not (yet) want to focus on possible relevant insights from the psychological literature itself.

debate, we believe that your focus when carrying out your literature review should rest on the literature written by *legal* academics.

> Determining what literature to look for specifically is not so hard if you already know your topic well. You might know about the presence of, for instance, (international and national) contributions that take a 'law and psychology' approach to the doctrine of 'mandatory warning' and that there is still room left for you to add to this debate. If this is the case, your literature review may focus on precisely that literature. We, however, recommend that you also briefly look at the disciplinary context (legal literature about mandatory warning, literature on the tort of negligence, and maybe literature on the duty of disclosure). This literature is however so substantial, that the process of collecting and processing these materials should be subjected to severe limitations.
>
> The situation where a researcher is interested in the interpretation of insurance policy terms, but only knows about a general textbook that spends a few pages on the interpretation of contracts in general, is quite a different one.[33] Here, we would recommend that you start searching for academic publications that relate to the interpretation of insurance policies. Again, include some materials that relate to the disciplinary context (literature on the doctrine of interpretation of contract terms, literature on insurance policies, and, for instance, also literature on the interpretation of commercial contracts) but realize that there is too much information on these themes to be mapped comprehensively. Also, you have to consider whether there is a European debate that is relevant to your topic. You may find that there is a European directive that prescribes that general terms in consumer contracts must be interpreted *contra proferentem*, meaning that you probably also have to dig into the international debate (if available) on this particular issue.[34] Contributions in, for instance, the literary sciences or psychology on explanation can be left aside though.
>
> As Den Hertogh (unpublished) has remarked before, "[i]t is also imaginable that no literature is available on your topic at all. Although this situation is unlikely to occur, this could present a problem for carrying out your literature review. In the few instances that this is actually the case, there is no other way than to establish links with contextual materials (either theoretical, conceptual, broader doctrinal, or interdisciplinary materials). If you for instance address a completely new topic like 3D-printing, you can approach it by looking through the lens of an existing legal field (intellectual property law)".

Whatever choices you make, we emphasize that it is important for you to reconsider them later on in your review process. What may seem to be highly relevant to your literature review in the first instance may upon further reflection appear uninteresting. But the opposite is also possible: when you come to know more about

---

33   This is exactly the situation that the majority of bachelor's and master's students find themselves in before embarking on a research assignment (see *paragraph 2.3*).

34   Of course, in the first instance, in general terms about the directive itself and not how it has been implemented in other countries. That information might become relevant if you finally decide to define a comparative research question.

your topic, you may find that a particular branch of literature you neglected earlier is in fact highly relevant to your enquiry.

3.7 Summary and key points

In this chapter, we presented the initial steps you need to take to start your literature review, which are to:

1. acknowledge the type of source that comprises a literature review, namely writings of scholars (secondary sources), which are not to be confused with legislation, court rulings, reports, opinions, regulation (primary sources). The latter can (must, even) be used during your research, but are not part of the focus of the literature review;
2. understand that secondary sources vary in scope, style, depth, objectiveness, and thus their contribution to your purposes must be evaluated in accordance with how analytically and thoroughly they discussed the topic;
3. recognize and classify the type of legal research that you will find (doctrinal, comparative, interdisciplinary, et cetera), so you can evaluate it accordingly later on (see *paragraph 5.2*);
4. delineate your topic before you start your literature review by going unsystematically through the literature to find an angle and have a sense of what to include in and what to exclude from your search, but be aware that more refining is likely to be necessary as you go through the literature review process;
5. remember to look for sources that touch upon your exact topic as their central discussion and avoid navigating around areas (psychology, sociology, et cetera) you do not know well enough;
6. formulate a *review* question that will guide you through the literature, but do not let that question keep you from finding the unexpected.

4 The systematic search for relevant literature

4.1   Introduction

Once you have established a review question and identified the types of literature most useful to you, you need to develop a systematic search strategy that enables you to identify and locate the widest range of published material in order to answer your *review* question in the most comprehensive way (Aveyard, 2010, p. 69). After all, without a thorough search strategy, your searching will be random and disorganized and you cannot be confident that you will have identified all the relevant scholarly works relating to your topic.

Both the difficulties and importance of developing a comprehensive search strategy are often underestimated by under- and postgraduates (Barry, 1997; Green & Macauley, 2007; Osborne, 2012, pp. 54-77).[1] To help convince you of the challenging nature of source collection, we will first reveal the major pitfalls of this process (*paragraph 4.2*). Against that backdrop, we will subsequently show you how to make the best possible effort to be as complete as we think you should be. Thinking carefully about first selection criteria (*paragraph 4.3*) and the *continuous* combination of different search techniques – searching in digital legal databases (*paragraph 4.4*), snowballing (*paragraph 4.5*) and a variety of additional techniques (*paragraph 4.6*) – are important here.

When reading this chapter, we urge you to keep in mind that doing research is a dynamic process. Your ideas about which literature is or is not relevant to your research will change during your research trajectory. Some of the literature you thought to include in your literature review may prove to be irrelevant or, the opposite, you might come across an interesting branch of literature that you did not think of in the first instance. When this happens, of course, you will need to revise your blueprint as necessary and collect more or different information (data) than you might have intended (compare Epstein & King, 2002, p. 54). To do so effectively, we believe it is important that you keep good records of your search process and that you carefully manage your sources (*paragraph 4.7*).

---

1   According to Greenhalgh (2010, p. 18), in the discipline of medicine and health care, many grant-giving bodies and publishers even *require* the involvement of information professionals (health librarians, clinical informationists, et cetera).

4.2   Collecting sources as a challenging research activity

You need to be aware that finding *all* of the (important) sources that are relevant to your enquiry is exceptionally difficult. In literature reviews we have seen in the past we hardly ever found complete coverage of the relevant secondary sources that were pertinent to the topic being addressed. Therefore, we were not surprised that an empirical study conducted in the social sciences found that by far the most common type of comment in examiners' reports on PhD theses was about coverage of the literature and the identification of errors such as the omission of references (Holbrook, Bourke, Fairburn, & Lovat, 2007). In this paragraph, we will point out the most important factors that make the process of source collection so difficult.[2]

Information overload

Over the past years, we have witnessed an immense growth (in sheer numbers) of national and international legal sources. The sea of legally relevant information is now almost infinite (Davidson, 2010, p. 563; Osborne, 2012, p. 11; Posner, 2008, p. 850). That often makes it impossible to oversee all the relevant sources relating to a specific legal theme. At the same time, this information overload also makes it more difficult to find those sources that are *specifically* relevant to a particular, delineated, review topic (compare Cohen & Olson, 2007, p. 13). You will sometimes have to search through hundreds of (lengthy) scholarly publications in search of that tiny bit of information that could be of actual relevance to your exact literature review topic.

Globalization, internationalization and Europeanization

If your topic is influenced by international or European law[3] or has an international or European character to begin with[4] (and you thus have to incorporate the international debate, see *paragraph 3.6*), achieving complete coverage is even more challenging. Sometimes, the influence of European or international law is concealed, so that there is a real chance that you completely miss this dimension (compare Westrik, 2016). But even if you are aware, you are not out of trouble yet. The scholar that usually focuses on domestic law will, as a result of a lack of experience and training in the international and European field, be less familiar with the beacons within this discourse. That may result in questions like 'do I have to look for relevant materials in each jurisdiction or can I make (and if so, how) meaningful selections here?', 'how can foreign sources be collected in a reliable way, taking into consideration the language barriers and unfamiliarity with databases and institutional systems applicable to other jurisdictions?',[5] 'if one consults publications by

---

2   This paragraph is based on Snel (2014, pp. 5-8) and Snel (2016, pp. 80-90).

3   *E.g.* product liability.

4   *E.g.* an investigation in the area of human rights, or a more theoretical theme such as constitutional dialogues.

5   We want to alert you to some general websites that may offer a starting point: <www.loc.gov/law/help/guide/nations.php> (offering links to relevant websites for

scholars from other jurisdictions, is it not then necessary to become aware of methodological issues addressed by literature on the methodology of comparative law?', and so on.

Digitalization and computerization

While generally considered a blessing, digitalization also brings challenges for the research process. Of course, there are the more obvious errors: the omission of relevant materials as a result of not consulting what is not published digitally (Greenberg, 2007, p. 2), access restrictions (Berring, 1997, p. 199; Van Dijck, 2016, p. 2), and the severe segmentation of information (Germain, 2007, pp. 148-151; Hutchinson, 2013, p. 9). But there are also more subtle difficulties you must overcome when searching online. Are you, for instance, aware of the pre-emptive decisions being made for you by the systems you are using (Berring, 1997, p. 199; Tjong Tjin Tai, 2013, p. 205; Van Opijnen, 2014)?[6] Do you know that while your keyword searches provide a list of matches in a database, they convey nothing about any relationship between the search results and other information in the database (Peoples, 2005, pp. 663-664)?[7] And do you realize that because some relevant literature might have been categorized using different keywords, it might not be identified by your specific keyword searches (Aveyard, 2010, pp. 81-82)?

> Montori, Wilczynski, Morgan, and Haynes (2004) undertook electronic searching for their literature review and describe how they frequently came across relevant literature by chance that had not been identified through their comprehensive electronic search strategy.

Preferences, assumptions or presuppositions

Preferences, assumptions or presuppositions on behalf of the researcher – or her supervisor(s)! – may also lead to the omission of relevant materials. Consciously or unconsciously, the researcher simply does not search for certain sources (for instance those that do not coincide with the ideas of the researcher, *collection bias*) or uses selection criteria (see *paragraph 4.3*) in such a way that materials that represent certain relevant ideas, interpretations or arguments structurally remain outside her search results (*selection bias*). In this context, (Van Gestel, 2013, p. 65) argued that "who searches for reasons to extend the existing catalogue of human rights, for more rights for victims in criminal proceedings, for more (European) regulation to

---

most countries) and <www.nylawglobal.org.globalex> (offering basic information about the legal systems of many countries).

6 According to Berring, "[t]he danger of the high-end [electronic] products is that each step in the research process that is carried out automatically by the front end system, is a step taken away from the purview of the researcher".

7 See also Van Opijnen (2014), who recently found that databases today still generally fail to classify information in a meaningful way. See also Van Gestel et al. (2012, p. 15).

effectively reduce environmental pollution, et cetera, will undoubtedly find arguments that provide support", as well as the other way around.[8]

Other pitfalls

Finally, there are a couple of other, more general threats to achieving complete coverage in the collection phase of your research trajectory. Firstly, sources may be omitted as a consequence of the speed and scale of legal or regulatory change.[9] Secondly, older sources are sometimes too easily dismissed as 'irrelevant' or even completely overlooked. And finally, trusting blindly in the choices made by others (by gathering the sources referred to in the contributions you already know of) may result in a situation where the researcher gets stuck with sources published by a limited group of scholars that often refer to each other (Korobkin, 1999, p. 866; Van Dijck, 2016, p. 18).

4.3   Searching is selecting

Before we present the techniques that may help you overcome these challenges, we would like to emphasize that, while we analytically distinguish between searching (this chapter) and making selections (**chapter 5** and **chapter 6**) for the purposes of this book, the selection process in fact starts as soon as you start your search process. Obviously, you will not be able to use all the results you get when you enter a particular keyword in a legal database for your literature review. Therefore, before designing your search strategy, you need to develop a strategy for managing the literature that allows you to quickly identify literature that is directly related to your topic and instantly discard literature that is irrelevant to you. Among other things, this will help you resist the temptation to include literature you find interesting but that only detracts from your review.

Establish inclusion and exclusion criteria

In order to do so, we believe it is important that you develop inclusion and exclusion criteria. The rationale for setting inclusion and exclusion criteria is twofold: (*1*) to give clear information about the remit of your review and (*2*) to focus your literature search (Aveyard, 2010, p. 72). Setting appropriate, clear and well-defined criteria assists you in keeping your study focused and ensures that you are not sidetracked by literature that is not strictly relevant to your review. At the same time, inclusion and exclusion criteria allow you to demonstrate (to the reader) the scope and detail of your review that you would not be able to demonstrate in the review question itself. In defining your criteria, let yourself be ruled by the wording of

---

8   Moreover, Peoples (2005) argued that the speed of searching electronic databases encourages researchers to rely on bits of rapidly retrieved text to support arguments that are often ill conceived and devoid of an enlightened, broad perspective.

9   This threat increases if the researcher focuses on an area of the law where things are currently moving quickly. Fisher et al. (2009, pp. 228-231) mention the field of (European) environmental law as an example.

your review topic. It is completely acceptable if, in the end, your inclusion and exclusion criteria are a combination of limits that are necessary to focus your search *and* pragmatic limitations that are required due to the time frame available to you (compare Van Dijck, 2016, p. 11). The important point is that you are able to *justify why* you used your particular set of criteria.

> The inclusion and exclusion criteria will be specific to your individual literature review, but there are a few, more general, recommendations we can make. If a pivotal event relevant to your review happened at a certain time, you might only be interested in literature published after that event ('include 1995 and onwards'). If you are only interested in local or national literature because you feel that your topic is mainly relevant to your own country, then you can state this in your inclusion criteria ('Dutch contributions only'). Equally, if you are interested in international literature, you should state why this is the case. If you are mainly interested in a specific aspect of the main topic, then you should state this in your inclusion and exclusion criteria as well ('exclude publications on *criminal* liability of governmental agencies for insufficient or inadequate supervision, include those on *civil* liability').

How to apply inclusion and exclusion criteria

Your inclusion and exclusion criteria may help you to quickly scan your search results. We recommend that you do apply your criteria loosely though. At this early stage of your research trajectory in particular, do include those sources of which you are not completely sure. Sometimes, you can complete your quick scan by only looking at the title of a source. However, research in the past has revealed that the focus of an article is often unclear from the title alone (Barroso et al., 2003; Evans, 2002). If that is the case, you should consult (if available) the abstract or passage in your search results where the keyword you searched is mentioned (compare Aveyard, 2010, pp. 83-84).[10] The abstract will give you a summary of the content of the article, therefore allowing you to make a better judgment with respect to the more content-related inclusion and exclusion criteria you established. However, be aware that when relying on abstracts it is still possible for you to miss relevant literature as abstracts can themselves also be unreliable sources for determining the exact focus of a paper.

4.4   Digital search through legal databases

Especially for the novice researcher who has grown up in a digital era, the most obvious technique to have recourse to is searching in digital legal databases (compare Dobinson & Johns, 2007, pp. 22-32). Before we explain the different steps that you should take in order to be systematic here, there are two things that should be emphasized. Firstly, despite the advantages of electronic searching, computerized search tools are never one hundred per cent comprehensive – for many different reasons, see *paragraph 4.2* – (compare Aveyard, 2010, p. 81; Tjong Tjin

---

10   HeinOnline, for instance, offers this possibility. In our experience, using this option will allow you to discard many publications that at first sight seemed relevant.

Tai, 2017, pp. 55-58). And secondly, from teaching legal research to both students and practitioners, it is clear that there is an element of talent and experience[11] involved in searching electronically (Dobinson & Johns, 2007, p. 30). Be aware that, generally, you will not be able to complete your search in half a day; in fact, if you are a novice researcher, it will only be when you finish your literature review that you are likely to feel really competent in using the search engines (Aveyard, 2010, p. 76).

Identify and get acquainted with relevant databases

The first thing we believe you should do in preparation for your electronic search is identify databases to which you have access and establish their relevance for your search strategy. It is important that you do not limit yourself to going through only a single database, not even if the content of that database seems all-encompassing or highly overlapping with other databases you can access. When you do have a clear picture of the databases you are going to consult, take your time to get acquainted with the particularities of these databases. How are they composed (what journals are incorporated in the databases)? How do they function (all databases operate slightly differently and it takes time and skill to learn how to use them effectively)? And what different search options do they offer (Boolean search and/or browsing, see hereafter; only search on title, or also on text, author, et cetera)?

> Tjong Tjin Tai (2017, pp. 55-56) distinguishes between (*1*) general purpose internet-based search engines (*Google*) – see *paragraph 4.6* – (*2*) specialized proprietary legal search engines that solely search through doctrinal literature and case law and provide access to proprietary databases of academic journals and case law publications, (*3*) proprietary academic search engines that search through academic literature (*Hein Online, Springer*), and (4) search engines offering access to public case law databases (*Hudoc*). Common databases that fall in the second and third categories are:[12]
> – *American Doctoral Dissertations*: access to American dissertations in many disciplines, including law, with links to full text if available;
> – *Beck-online*: portal for German law, holding both primary and secondary sources;
> – *Dalloz.fr*: portal for French law, holding both primary and secondary sources;
> – *Directory of Open Access Journals*: access to journals in all subject fields, partly searchable at article level;
> – *Ebrary*: e-books in various disciplines from leading scholarly publishers;
> – *EUR*-Lex: European Union legal material, documents and legislative procedures;

---

11 We therefore believe electronic searching is a skill that you can and need to practice and practice.

12 A more complete overview of relevant sources for each jurisdiction and how to use them is covered in other publications, see Mersky and Dunn (2002), Hutchinson (2010), and Thomas and Knowles (2006).

- *Heinonline*: portal to all kinds of (retrospective) legal materials;
- *JSTOR*: archive of scholarly journals from different disciplines, including law. Recent volumes are not included;
- *Jura*: legal database containing Belgian legislation, case law, and references to literature;
- *Kluwer Navigator*: comprehensive legal database with Dutch materials published by Wolters Kluwer;
- *Legal Intelligence*: portal for Dutch, European and international law containing free legal sources as well as content from publishers;
- *LexisNexis*: articles of a large number of newspapers and journals;
- *Netherlands Central Catalogue*: metadata of books and periodicals in more than 400 libraries in the Netherlands;
- *Oxford Journals*: access to journal articles of Oxford University Press;
- *Oxford Public International law*: access to the Max Planck Encyclopedia of Public International Law and Oxford Historical Treaties;
- *Rapid*: press releases of the European Commission;
- *SAGE Journals Online*: access to journals of publisher Sage;
- *SSRN*: devoted to the rapid worldwide dissemination of information. It contains abstracts and full texts of published articles, book chapters, and working papers;[13]
- *Taylor and Francis Online*: journals of publisher Taylor & Francis;
- *UN iLibrary*: access to publications, published by the United Nations Secretariat, and its funds and programs;
- *Westlaw Next*: legal information portal with international and national materials;
- *Wiley*: scholarly journals in several disciplines including law of publisher Wiley.

Librarians usually distinguish two different database models that offer distinct search facilities (Dobinson & Johns, 2007, pp. 29-31; Mart, 2010, pp. 221-223). Some databases are designed to be *browsed*. Browsing means relying on the structure of the database where navigation is done by using an alphabetical list, a table of contents, a date range, or an index, simply by using mouse clicks to find a particular document. Other databases are designed to be *searched*. In this case, computer algorithms translate the keywords or a combination of keywords the researcher enters in various search fields into a list of results from the large body of information that is included in the database ('Boolean search'-model).[14] While

---

13 Van Dijck (2016, pp. 7-8) addressed the advantages and disadvantages of using SSRN. He mentions that it is important to keep in mind that the papers in the SSRN database can contain various types of uploads; from completed, reviewed and published works, to first versions of working papers. While SSRN does have a review process regarding each version that is uploaded or modified, it is not clear what this review process actually entails.

14 Dobinson and Johns (2007, p. 30) remark that "[t]here may be an assumption that Boolean searching obviates the need for an index. But the opposite is true. The more overwhelming the information available online, the more important the proper indexing of a database". See also Bast and Pyle (2001), who argue that because of the vol-

there are some databases that also apply the 'index'-model,[15] legal scholars currently have to rely mainly on the 'Boolean search'-model. Therefore, it is important that you take your time to develop a comprehensive list of appropriate keywords that capture the essence of your research topic and allow you to identify suitable references (compare Clinch & Mullan, 2010, pp. 11-13).

Establish keywords

Brainstorm as many keywords as you can think of that represent your review question.[16] In general, we recommend that you, on the one hand, define search terms that are specific – directly related to your (narrow) research topic – but, on the other hand, also define more general search terms that can function as a 'safety net' (compare Parise, 2010, p. 8; Tijssen, 2009, p. 62).[17] Try to think of synonyms and alternative terms[18] and try to match your language to that of the terminology you encounter in the sources you already know of. Do not forget to include names of judicial opinions or leading authors and publications in your field, as that has proven to be a very effective method of narrowing down a search without unwittingly excluding important hits (Dobinson & Johns, 2007, p. 31). Be prepared to experiment and to amend your keywords as your research progresses. You may find, as you go through the literature, that there are other ways of describing your subject you did not think of before (Bryman, 2008, p. 100).

> In defining your keywords, you should pay attention to every detail (compare Van Opijnen, 2014, pp. 274-278, 287-290, 297-299, 310-324). If, for instance, you search for literature that refers to a judicial opinion of the European Court of Justice number C-484/08, then what you will find may depend on whether you searched for 'C-484/08', 'C-484-08', 'C/484/08', or the case name without the number. The same applies to the search for literature on, for instance, self-defense. Whether you enter 'self-defense', 'self defense', or 'self-defensing' matters for the hits you get. Also, see whether the databases you selected support the * or $ function. If that is the case, that function will enable you to identify all possible endings of the key term you write. For example, 'nurs*' will identify articles containing, 'nurse', 'nursing', 'nurses', and so on.

---

ume of legal materials available online, Boolean or free text searching may not always be the most efficient way to proceed.

15   Examples are AccessUN (UN documents and publications), Current Index to Legal Periodicals, Foreign Law Guide, and Global Jurist.

16   Research in medicine has revealed that when more than 2 or 3 search terms are used, the efficiency of searches improves substantially (Hoogendam, Robbee, & Overbeke, 2008).

17   In line with what we discussed in *paragraph 3.6*.

18   It may be helpful to use a legal thesaurus to identify alternative words, such as <www.thesaurus.com/browse/legal>.

Execute your search

Once you are happy with your keywords, they can be entered into the databases you selected. This is not simply a matter of entering the separate keywords you established in an open search field one after the other. Again, many choices and judgment calls have to be made (compare Clinch, 2001). One of us previously found a few considerations that may help you structure this search process (Snel, 2016, p. 123). Firstly, it is advisable to start your search at the advanced searching option of the database rather than to undertake a basic search, as the basic search is very limited and is likely to yield an overwhelming number of hits that you will not be able to go through systematically. To the extent possible, try to set up your search so that it already takes some of your inclusion and exclusion criteria into account (*i.e.* make sure – if that was one of your criteria – that only publications that appeared after a particular date come up in the search results). We recommend that you then start entering your separate keywords (except for obvious combinations, combine those directly) in the field that allows you to search through the *text* (not *title*) of the sources included in the database. Some of these searches will directly result in a list with a manageable number of sources that you can go through immediately. In other cases, the keyword you enter may result in too many (also irrelevant) hits. If this is the case, we recommend that you narrow down your search by making clever use of the advanced search syntax options the database supports (for an overview, see table 4.1). If you still get too many results, you may consider resorting to only searching through *titles* and/or *abstracts* (if the option is available) of the sources incorporated in the database.

Table 4.1 Advanced search syntax

Boolean Logic	AND	liability and tort	finds both words in the same record.
	OR	slander or libel	finds either word in same record.
	NOT	bankruptcy not liquidation	finds records which mention the first word but not second.
Proximity Indicators Note: these vary across databases.	Phrase Searching	"duty of care"	forces the database to search a string of words as a phrase.
	/s	circumstances /s mitigating	retrieves records which have both words in the same sentence.
	/p	defendant /p bail	retrieves records which have both words in the same paragraph.

	/n	market /5 share	retrieves words which appear with 'n' (in this instance 5) words of each other.
	pre/n	filing pre/5 bankrupt!	retrieves first word within 'n' words of second keyword in the order specified.
Truncation and Wildcards Note: symbols vary across databases.	Truncation	Lexis, LexisNexis AU and Westlaw use!; other databases *	searches for alternate endings of words eg. negligen! retrieves negligence, negligent, negligently.
	Wildcard	Lexis, LexisNexis AU and Westlaw use *; other databases ?	replaces a single character eg. defen*e retrieves defense, defence.
Nesting	(brackets)	(World trade organi?ation OR WTO) and intellectual property.	use brackets when your search strategy contains more than one Boolean operator. Place the synonyms in brackets.

4.5   Snowballing

To be complete, it is indispensable that you also thoroughly and sophisticatedly apply the technique that is usually referred to as 'snowballing' (also called 'reference tracking' or 'citation chaining'). This technique is commonly used, important, and hence widely accepted among legal scholars (Cohen & Olson, 2007, p. 14; Tjong Tjin Tai, 2017, pp. 52-53). It entails scrutinizing the reference lists of publications you already know of or that you have found in the legal databases for further references that may be useful to you, and then repeating this process with the newly identified materials. For the successful application of this technique, we believe it is important that you – as soon as possible – try to identify the sources that are 'key' to your literature review and work outwards from there. There is not much use in going through the references of a source that only indirectly or slightly touches upon your research topic. In particular, when you come across a monograph (which – as we have said before – is characterized by the fact that it usually has a high density of references with respect to the topic it addresses) you should operate meticulously.[19]

---

19   Moreover, you may benefit from the fact that you get a quick overview of your project context, as these sources usually also pay a lot of attention to that context.

The most pressing question that arises in relation to the technique of reference tracking is when the researcher may bring this process, which is, in principle, infinite, to a halt. As a rule of thumb, we believe that you may stop scrutinizing the references of the most recently discovered publications when, say, five consecutive 'key publications' do not result in the identification of new relevant materials (the 'saturation principle', see Van Dijck, 2016, p. 10). If that moment just does not seem to come, you might wonder whether your topic is delineated enough. If that is the case, we recommend that you return to the drawing board rather than keep trying to take sand to the beach.

An additional benefit of snowballing, is that the fact that others have referred to a publication and the exact way in which they did so, may tell you a great deal about the support, authority and quality that a particular source enjoys and therefore also about the possible relevance it may have for your enquiry (for elaboration, see **chapter 5**).[20] A big disadvantage, however, is that snowballing may lead to infinite regression. Anyone who has already been involved in legal scholarship will immediately recognize that after you have become immersed in a particular research field, almost everything you come across will conjure up associations with your research topic. If you keep discovering new interesting alleys, however, you will never be able to reach your destination.

4.6   Additional techniques

It should be noted that even the combination of searching in digital legal databases and snowballing will probably fail to identify all the literature relating to your review topic. Greenhalgh and Peacock (2005) have therefore emphasized the importance of combining many approaches for identifying the appropriate literature when undertaking a literature search. We distinguish four additional techniques that we recommend you employ besides searching in digital legal databases and snowballing: (*1*) searching the open web, (*2*) searching relevant journals by hand, (*3*) author searching, and (*4*) consulting experts in your field.

Searching the open web

There is one thing to be sure of: legal scholars (including novices) *do* rely on Google when conducting legal research (compare Osborne, 2016, p. 407).[21] Whilst we definitely do not advise against it – we believe in the benefits of searching the open web, also in the context of academic scholarship – we do want to mention a few things you should take into consideration when doing so. Firstly, searching through Google on keywords will generally result in too many hits to go through systematically.

---

20   You should realize that references might serve various purposes. Determination of the purpose that a particular reference serves may give you an important indication about whether the reference can be of value for your literature review or not.

21   By now, articles and books have been written on how lawyers may use Google. See for instance Levitt and Rosch (2010), Neacsu (2007), and Tsai and Minick (2009).

Van Dijck (2016, pp. 14-15) provides an interesting example on the search process you may undergo when you are interested in the role of apologies in tort law: "An automatic response of many novice researchers (worldwide) is to search on the Internet, for example Google, using keywords such as 'apologies', 'legal', and 'tort law'. The hits on the first page yield possibly interesting papers, including those by Caroll,[22] Ho,[23] Rachlinski et al.,[24] and Robbennolt.[25] However, there are many pages that follow that may (and do) also provide relevant publications. Because of this, it is often confusing to novices what the next step should be. Some start to look for additional publications by going to the next page with hits on Google; others start a new search with different keywords, or they start reading the 'hits' on the first page".

Secondly, you should be aware that Google in no way discerns between academic and all kind of other forms of information. Google merely finds sites, but does not evaluate them. Remember that anyone can put information on the web, so always maintain an extra critical attitude towards materials found there (see also *paragraph 5.2*).

Thirdly, there is a lot of information that Google cannot show. The majority of law journals and publishers do not (at least not yet) participate fully in the open access movement. That means that many scholarly works – that you should rely on when doing a literature review – are subjected to (sometimes strict) access restrictions and therefore may not show up in your Google search results. Seen in conjunction, this makes us believe that it would not be a good idea to rely on Google for the systematic retrieval of information on a particular topic (compare Van Dijck, 2016, p. 15). Rather, as presented here, we believe that it should be used as an additional technique.[26]

As it focuses on scholarly literature, using Google Scholar solves the first problem we identified. This does not, however, solve our second problem. While Google Scholar claims to rank documents the way researchers do, weighing the full text of each document, where it was published, who it was written by, as well as how often

---

22   Carroll's *'Apologies as a Legal Remedy'* (2013).
23   Ho and Liu's *'Does Sorry Work? The Impact of Apology Laws on Medical Malpractice'* (2011).
24   Rachlinski, Guthrie and Wistrich's *'Contrition in the Courtroom: Do Apologies Affect Adjudication?'* (2013).
25   Robbennolt's *'Apologies and Legal Settlement: An Empirical Examination'* (2003).
26   When doing so, at least in our experience, you will always find something that is relevant to your topic that you have not come across before. Perhaps this is because Google's searching patterns are much more sophisticated and interactive than legal information systems. Google works by providing a hit list that is relevance-ranked according to a combination of the search terms and in order of other web pages which point to that document. Google's hit lists are dynamic and determined by the importance given to specific web pages by the Internet community. This ensures that any search second-guesses the information the researcher is looking for.

and how recently it has been cited in other scholarly literature,[27] it has been subjected to severe criticism: it does not have access to as many academic journals as the more subject-specific databases and does not have an advanced searching facility (Aveyard, 2010, p. 75), searches are said to be unreliable for the results they produce, there is a lack of transparency about the search process, and the system is susceptible to being manipulated in order to get more citations of an article (Van Dijck, 2016, p. 6).

Searching relevant journals by hand

After identifying a substantial number of relevant research materials, we believe it to be useful to further scrutinize the journals that may hold materials relevant to your literature review. If you have been able to identify that many of the key articles to your review are located in a small number of journals, it might be useful to search these journals by hand (going through the contents pages) to see whether you can identify other relevant articles that have not been identified through other search strategies. Though cumbersome and time-consuming, this method has positive side-effects, such as making sure you also include the most recent information and obtain a more general familiarity with the literature (Tjong Tjin Tai, 2017, pp. 54-55).

Author searching

The same principle applies to author searching. If you find that many of your key articles are written by the same author(s), it may be useful to carry out an author search in order to identify whether the author(s) has (or have) published other work that has not been identified in the electronic search (Aveyard, 2010, p. 83; Van Dijck, 2016, p. 16). This might also lead you to work in progress. Several platforms allow for searches of researchers and their publications. Apart from the website of the institution at which a particular scholar is located, examples are *ResearchGate* and *Academia.edu*.

Consultation of experts and supervisors

In a field as overwhelming and complex as legal scholarship, asking your supervisor (or another expert), colleagues, and people you trust has always been a preferred source of information. Asking around can no longer be considered sufficient for a search for information, but can any search really be complete without it? As we believe the answer should be no, we strongly recommend that you also ask your supervisor and/or other experts in the field you are interested in to point you to sources you might have missed.

---

27   See <https://scholar.google.com/intl/en/scholar/about.html>.

4.7   Keep track of your search and manage your references

In designing your search strategy and carrying out your search, we believe it is important that you keep track of everything you have done – an *audit trail* – and that you manage your references (compare Aveyard, 2010, pp. 80-81; Bryman, 2008, p. 101). Whilst keeping track of your search and managing your references may seem like a time-consuming and boring thing to do, we ask you to believe us when we say that you will regain that time and you will benefit from it in many other ways as your research project advances.

> Firstly, by keeping track of your search activities and managing your references, you will ensure that you are systematic. Secondly, doing so may prevent you from doing work twice. If your audit trail indicates that you have already searched through database A using a particular keyword, you will be prevented from doing the same thing once more (including the whole process of going through all hits you get). Thirdly, if you need to revise your search, it will be easy to pick up where you left off. Fourthly, keeping an audit trail and thus being able to show it, gives confidence to your readers (and yourself!). And finally, it makes it easy for others (for instance your supervisor) to correct you or steer you in the right direction.[28]

The only thing you will need to do is to be disciplined in actually recording what you are doing. We recommend that you at least record (*1*) the inclusion and exclusion criteria you established, (*2*) the databases you selected, (*3*) the keywords you defined, (*4*) the exact (combination) of keywords you entered in the different databases including the date on which you did so, (*5*) a demonstration of the success of each search query (*i.e.* 120 hits, twenty selected), and (*6*) the additional techniques you used and the results they yielded (compare Baude et al., 2017, p. 47). We have provided an example of an audit trail of an electronic search in *table 4.2*.

Apart from keeping an audit trail, also manage your references. Before you begin to search, consider how you are going to manage the references you identify. Whether you record your references on a computer or on paper, it is vitally important to back up all your records and keep them in a safe place from the moment you begin the searching process. We recommend that you at least keep an electronic copy and enter the essentials in a reference manager, such as *Endnote* or *Refworks* (or create your own in *Excel*). While this may seem haphazard, we enjoy the benefits of it on a daily basis.[29]

---

28   Whether you should incorporate (a summary of) your audit trail in your final text and in what way, we cannot tell. It depends on your assignment, your own and your supervisor's preferences, and/or the medium you want to publish in. Remember though that if you are not *required* to keep track, that does not relieve you of your duty to do so.

29   Furthermore, if you start this process at the beginning of your research project you will only have to update the information in your reference manager once you find new sources. Especially combined with the handy feature of being able to add PDF files to the references, this ensures that your personal library will grow with information hand-picked by yourself throughout your research.

Table 4.2   Example of an audit trail

Audit trail electronic search

Include	Specific techniques, published journal articles and monographs
Exclude	Philosophical and theoretical works, non-published materials

Database 1 – Hein Online

Date	Keywords	Hits	Selected
July 2017	(text) methods AND (text) research	211	55
July 2017	(text) research AND (text) methodology	498	77
July 2017	(text) doctrinal AND (text) method*	43	21
August 2017	(text) "literature review" AND (text) method*	28	12
December 2017	(text) meth* AND (text) legal AND (text) science	87	33

Database 2 – Westlaw Next

Date	Keywords	Hits	Selected
July 2017	(text) methods AND (text) research	98	25
July 2017	(text) research AND (text) methodology	233	51
July 2017	(text) doctrinal AND (text) method*	15	7
October 2017	(text) "literature review" AND (text) method*	25	12
October 2017	(text) meth* AND (text) legal AND (text) science	33	15

4.8   Summary and key points

In this chapter, we shared strategies that will make your search for literature systematic and consequently will enhance the chance that you do not miss any relevant scholarly works. These strategies comprise the following aspects:

1. be aware of the common problems that lead to incomplete coverage of the literature, namely the excess of available information that is not filtered according

to its quality, the current process of legislation that extrapolates the boundaries of a country, the issues concerning the digitalization of information, the researcher's assumptions that might blind her to other possible approaches to the topic, and the rapid changes in the law that may lead to the premature dismissal of important sources;

2. develop a justifiable set of inclusion and exclusion criteria when you start searching for the literature;

3. get acquainted with the digital databases, in order to know which ones to use and how to best manage their search tools;

4. develop keywords that represent the crucial aspects of your topic;

5. track the references of the sources you found or already knew about in order to find works related to your area (snowballing);

6. use as additional techniques (not primary ones): (a) a search on the open web (for example, Google search), but be careful to discern between reliable contents and those that are not and remember that many journals do not index their content on the open internet; (b) a specific search in a journal that appeared to be relevant in your initial enquiry; (c) a specific search for an author who seemed to be influential in your topic; (d) a consultation of experts and your supervisor to make sure that you are not missing any important material;

7. register your search activities (the databases you used, on what date you accessed them, the search terms, the number of hits, your inclusion/exclusion criteria, the techniques employed).

5 Critical appraisal of the literature

5.1 Introduction

Your systematic search will result in a list of materials that are potentially relevant to your literature review. Frequently, either one of two things happens at this point. There is a group of students that starts reading the literature in a relaxed way and a group that instantly begins drafting the review. We actually do not think you should do either. Rather, we recommend that you take your time to get to know your literature well by scrutinizing – or as we will refer to it here, by *critically appraising* – the materials you found. Whilst executing this step comprehensively is time-consuming, doing so will avoid potentially stressful situations, will prevent you from forgetting about important issues, will help you speed up in developing a synthesis (**chapter 6**), and, ultimately, will enhance the quality of your review.[1]

In this chapter, paragraph by paragraph, we will equip you with an appraisal tool that should help you go through this process systematically.[2] To get you started, we will first present an overview of criteria that may be used for appraising legal literary sources (*paragraph 5.2*). As, in most cases, you will not be able to carefully read and reread *all* your search results, we will explain how best to use these criteria to further refine your literature to a manageable amount of publications that are 'key' to your review (*paragraph 5.3*). From there, we will provide you with some guidelines on how to appraise the sources that survived this selection process at a deeper, methodological, level (*paragraph 5.4*).

When going through the literature with the purpose of determining its relevance and (methodological) quality, you might as well start distilling and organizing information that you probably will need later on. Therefore, we will also provide you with suggestions on how to take notes and how to categorize all the information you come across logically (*paragraph 5.5*) as well as on how to assign provisional codes to all of that information (*paragraph 5.6*).

---

1   We thus urge you not to underestimate this recommendation on how to go about the literature, as accomplishing the critical appraisal task is the only way to find your path within the body of knowledge (compare Holbrook et al., 2007, p. 348).

2   Inspired by the many appraisal tools (Katrak, Bialocerkowski, Massy-Westropp, Kumar, & Grimmer, 2004 located a total of 121 tools) present in other disciplines.

5.2   Appraisal criteria

Not all information is necessarily equivalent. You will need to keep a sharp eye out for the believability of whatever information you find, wherever you find it. There are several criteria that may help determine whether you should include a particular publication in your literature review (*paragraph 5.3*) and estimate the weight or impact that the publication has in addressing your review topic (*paragraph 5.4*). We will distinguish between what we will refer to as 'the relevance-criterion', 'formal criteria', and 'substantive or methodological criteria'. We elaborate these aspects in what follows.

Relevance-criterion

The relevance-criterion is probably the most important of all appraisal criteria. You will have previously delineated your broader review topic so that it now has a tight focus (*paragraph 3.5*). You now need to make sure that the literature you use for the construction of your review fits this close focus. Under this criterion, you will thus examine to what extent each piece of literature is related to the center of your review topic. Ask yourself whether the source exactly addresses the issue(s) you are interested in, whether it only marginally touches upon your subject, or whether it mainly contains interesting contextual insights. As a rule of thumb, of course, a publication that discusses your topic as its central issue will be the most relevant to your review.

Formal criteria

While important, the relevance-criterion conveys nothing about the quality of a particular publication. Of course, you will want to focus your literature review on high-quality publications and leave out those that are of poor quality. Even though a quality judgment is preferably based on a substantive assessment of a text, it will – depending on your topic – sometimes simply be impossible for you to carefully read and scrutinize all the materials that meet the relevance-criterion. If that is the case, you must find a way that can help you make a first selection more quickly. This is where the formal criteria that we introduce below come in (compare Van Dijck, 2016, p. 11). By formal, we mean anything that is not related to the content of the writing itself. We distinguish between (*1*) recency, (*2*) author reputation, (*3*) publication status, (*4*) usage of the source by other scholars, and (*5*) bibliometrics. Before we discuss those in more depth, we would like to emphasize the fact that formal criteria, while indicative, can *never* be decisive for the actual quality of a work of legal scholarship.

Recency
As Van Dijck (2016, p. 11) also stated, it can be worthwhile to *focus* your literature review on recent works rather than on older publications. That is especially true if the law itself has undergone major changes and some of the older literature still

focuses on the old legal regime.[3] The recency criterion may also be helpful if you are addressing a topic that has received excessive scholarly attention and/or when there is a lot of repetition of arguments and interpretations within the scholarly debate. Also, you will often find that a single author has addressed a particular topic a couple of times over a period of time. As the newer pieces may repeat or even correct what the author wrote earlier before something new is said, it may sometimes be acceptable to focus only on the latest work(s).

Author reputation

In nearly all legal fields, there are authorities. These, generally, are the authors who are frequently cited in academic debates and classrooms. If you are exploring a new area and do not know who the authorities are, what might help is to (*a*) check the authors who took part in a reputable book series in your field (*i.e.* the *Asser*-series for Dutch Law), (*b*) look for the author's affiliation (with a prestigious institute or other affiliation), (*c*) check whether the author is cited by other authors (see hereafter), and (*d*) consider the track record of the author (previous works). When relying on author reputation, it is important that you try to find out whether the author has the necessary experience and qualifications to undertake research in *the area you are interested in*, rather than to look at the general experience and qualifications of the author.

Publication status

The status of a particular publication may also serve as an appraisal criterion. There are a couple of aspects to this criterion. Firstly, generally speaking, articles and books that are published are preferred to non-published works (Van Dijck, 2016, p. 11). Secondly, as we already stated in *paragraph 3.3*, reflective books and articles may be preferred to textbooks, and substantive pieces are preferred to short opinion pieces or essays. Thirdly, and this is more tricky, you could rely on the publication outlet. Several institutions classify journals; for example, the ranking promoted by the *Washington and Lee University School of Law*[4] in the United States, *Qualis* in Brazil, *Siems World Law Journal Ranking* in the United Kingdom, and the *ERA journal ranking list* in Australia.[5] Generally, articles published in journals with a higher position in such ranks meet academic thresholds and therefore tend to be of sufficient or even outstanding quality. However, especially in many parts of continental Europe, explicit journal rankings are absent. That does not mean that, implicitly[6] of course, the scholarly community considers some journals to be more

---

3   Be aware though that this literature, especially if it took a more reflective stance on the issue you are interested in, may still be of value to your research project!

4   Van Dijck (2016, p. 12) states "[h]owever, this ranking is biased towards legal journals based in the U.S. For example, the well-respected *European Law Journal*, is ranked well below the *Sports Lawyers Journal*".

5   Other rankings include Google Scholar Metrics, ExpressO, and SCImago.

6   As Van Dijck (2016, p. 12) remarks, these "[r]ankings exist mainly in the minds of the researchers. For example, publishers such as Cambridge University Press, Oxford University Press, Hart Publishing, and Edward Elgar Publishing are well-respected book publishers, but certainly not the only ones".

reputable than others. For book publishers, we only know of the existence of a Norwegian ranking[7] and a modified version thereof created by two Belgian scholars (Svacina & Van Gompel, 2012, p. 335).[8]

> There can be no doubt that the internet also contains a wealth of information that may be useful for legal scholars. However, it has to be acknowledged that unlike publishers and journals, websites are unregulated and it is possible for anybody to publish anything on an internet site. You are therefore recommended to adopt a critical attitude towards any website you encounter. Fink (2010) suggests that you should ask the following questions: (1) who supports the site? (2) when was it last updated?, and (3) what authority do the authors of the site have? According to Bryman (2008, p. 97), the following points are worth considering: "Who is the author of the site and what is their motive for publishing? Where is the site located? The URL can help you here. Is it an academic site (.ac) or a government site (.gov), a non-commercial organization (.org) or a commercial one (.com or .co)?"

Usage of a source by other scholars
Another way to get a sense of the potential quality of a source without scrutinizing it is to see if and in what ways other scholars have referred to it. You will be able to verify this through snowballing (*paragraph 4.5*) or by entering the title of a particular source in the 'text'-field of one or more digital legal databases (the amount of results you will get will reveal how often others have referred to the particular source). When relying on this indicator, you should not only count the citations but also look for the reason why another author referred to this source. Was it with praise or was it, rather, critical?

Bibliometrics
Finally, although uncommon and underdeveloped in legal scholarship compared to many other academic disciplines,[9] the legal scholar can still benefit from using bibliometrics to help identify the potential quality of a particular source. There are journals and databases that count views, downloads, and/or citations. The idea behind this criterion is that the most viewed, downloaded, and cited papers tend to be the ones providing the most interesting contributions to a particular field that you should not miss in your literature review. Examples of legal databases that make use of some form of bibliometrics – imperfect though they are – are *SSRN* (views and downloads counted) and *HeinOnline* (citations).

---

7   Norwegian Scientific Index. See: www.cristin.no/english/.
8   For all kinds of reasons, such as the amount of submissions they get, the composition of the editorial board, whether they are peer-reviewed or not, et cetera. Van Gestel (2015, pp. 264-288) convincingly shows that the fact that a particular journal is peer-reviewed does not, in itself, say a lot though. There are many different forms of peer review and it can be done thoroughly, but also superficially.
9   For good reasons, see Van Leeuwen (2013) and the German Wissenschaftsrat (2012).

Substantive criteria

While formal criteria might give you an indication of the quality of a work of legal scholarship, its quality is ultimately determined by its content. In the past, scholars have proposed substantive quality standards that works of legal scholarship should meet. From that, we learn that different types of research (see *paragraph 3.3* and *paragraph 3.4*) are to be examined using different standards (compare Aveyard, 2010, pp. 100-118).[10] Unfortunately, in this book, we will not be able to provide a detailed picture of the quality standards that apply to all forms of legal scholarship and how they work in practice. We confine ourselves to providing an overview – which we admit is too brief – of the standards mentioned by other scholars. When standing before your appraisal task, we recommend you – at least – immerse yourself in the works we refer to in this book.

Doctrinal legal research
Snel (2017b) recently mapped the state of the art on the quality standards that apply to doctrinal legal scholarship. The conclusion was that doctrinal legal research should meet the following quality standards. It should have a clearly and precisely formulated research question and persuasively justify how answering that question contributes significantly to the existing body of knowledge, as well as employ adequate and justified methods of data collection and processing. Subsequently, the answer to the research question must be accompanied by correct references, it must be accurate (it must actually be answered), balanced (complete and correctly weighed view of the source materials), and credible (each statement of it must be credible). Finally, the author must have (persuasively) justified the choices that were made during the research project and must have constrained the influence of her own assumptions and presuppositions in relation to the topic addressed (explication of normative stance).

Comparative law and legal history
Comparative law and legal history are closely connected to doctrinal legal research. Therefore, we believe that the criteria for doctrinal legal research are also valid for these types of scholarship. The distinctive nature of comparative law and legal history however implies that additional criteria apply. Comparative studies[11] should not only be explicit about the methods of data-collection, but also about the methods of comparison (functional method, deep-level, et cetera). Furthermore, the selection of countries and the so-called *tertium comparationis* (the common quality of the two things being compared) needs to be explained. Finally, in comparative law projects, it is important that the author's own perceptions (from her own jurisdiction) are controlled. Studies in the field of legal history, according to Nelson (1982), also need to (*i*) be comprehensible in view of the language the author chooses to use (the language of law, of history or a third new one), (*ii*) be factually

---

10   The quality of doctrinal legal research, for instance, is not measured by the exact same standards as empirical legal research.
11   Based on the publications of Van Hoecke (2015), Samuel (2014), Husa (2006), Dannemann (2006), Hirschl (2005), and Frankenberg (2006).

accurate (but the reviewer must pay attention to the possibility of multiple inter-pretations of the same data), and (*iii*) contribute to the area, either by providing new insights, employing new methods, exploring source materials that have not been explored before, or fostering new lines of thought for further investigation.

Empirical legal research and 'law and' studies

In 2002, Epstein and King examined 231 empirical legal publications published in the United States law reviews between 1990 and 2000. To be able to do so, they explicated rules that could improve each component of the empirical legal research design. Firstly, as is the case with the former types of legal research, there must be a research question that demonstrably contributes to existing knowledge and has some importance for the real world. Secondly, empirical legal studies must theorize (contain a reasoned and precise speculation) about possible answers to that research question that are, in turn, used to generate observable implications (things that can be detected in the real world if the theory is right, or hypotheses). Thirdly, empiri-cal legal studies must control for rival hypotheses. Fourthly, the tools used to mea-sure hypotheses must be both reliable (the extent to which it is possible to replicate a measurement, reproducing the same value – regardless of whether it is the right one – on the same standard for the subject, at the same time) and valid (the extent to which a reliable measure reflects the underlying concept being measured). Finally, empirical legal studies must clearly identify the population of interest, col-lect as much data as feasible, record the process by which data come to be observed, and collect data in a manner that avoids selection bias.

> In other disciplines, a lot has been written on quality standards, especially in relation to the validity criterion. Several subcriteria are distinguished (internal validity, exter-nal validity, construct validity, face validity, evaluative validity, theoretical validity, and so on). We provide an example that relates to two of the most commonly men-tioned subcriteria. Is the claim that the Supreme Court has altered its attitude with regard to the scope of the duty of care of a house buyer in a particular judicial opin-ion valid in the sense that the Supreme Court itself really intended to change its attitude within the opinion (a matter of internal validity)? Is the claim about the scope of the duty of care of a house buyer that was made on the basis of three judi-cial opinions addressing this issue valid in the sense that the claim holds if other judicial opinions of the Supreme Court (and possibly even other – lower – courts) are consulted (a matter of external validity)?

Case notes

Case notes can usually be typified as a specific form of doctrinal legal research (sometimes with elements of the other types of legal scholarship). Of course, the criteria we discussed above also apply to case notes. The specific character of the case note however means that several additional quality standards apply. The empirical study of Van Dijck (2011) shows that the quality of a case note is also determined by the extent to which it displays the implications of the verdict, exam-ines the verdict in light of the higher law, uses well-developed criteria to reach a judgment about the opinion, and is not limited to the individual case (comes to generalizable insights even though triggered by a specific case).

For *jurisprudence* and '*Law and*' research, we did not find any written substantive criteria. We believe that enquiries in the field of *jurisprudence* must largely comply with similar standards as doctrinal research. '*Law and*' investigations must conform to both standards of legal research and the standards of the discipline with which law is combined. For this type of research, however, we also believe it is important that the researcher explains and justifies how exactly the connection between the legal and other discipline is made.

5.3   Refining the literature that will comprise the review

A common flaw of literature reviews is the researcher's effort to squeeze in all the sources she found without an assessment of their quality and appropriateness to the scope of the review (Bryman, 2008, p. 99). Even though you have established inclusion and exclusion criteria to filter your search results (*paragraph 4.2*), generally, your search strategy will not suffice to ensure the quality of the sources and their relatedness and relevance to your topic (compare Aveyard, 2010, p. 93). Your list of references will probably still contain materials that are of poor quality or that are irrelevant to your tight review topic.[12] The first step of the critical appraisal stage should thus be aimed at further filtering out the materials that are most useful to your review topic.[13] We recommend that you go through the list of references you collected and try to reduce it to a number of publications that are 'key' to your research project without reading everything thoroughly. What you, as a novice researcher, are aiming for – we are aware that we might be oversimplifying things a bit here – is an initial list of about twenty publications[14] that will form the core of your literature review.

We think you should generally be able to make this provisional selection on the basis of the relevance criterion and the more formal quality criteria we presented in *paragraph 5.2*. The first thing you should do is apply the relevance-criterion to slim down your list. The question you should ask yourself here ('is this literature relevant to my review?') can in most cases be answered by going through the abstract, table of contents, introduction and conclusion of the references you collected. Only if you are still in doubt, will you probably have to scan through the complete text of a source. We urge you not to feel disconcerted about removing sources that seem prestigious but are not relevant to your work.

---

12 For example, at first glance, a research paper might appear to address your review topic directly; however, on closer inspection you realize that the scope of the paper is very different from what your initial assessment had led you to believe and in fact has only indirect relevance or no relevance at all to your review topic.

13 Studies have shown that novice researchers find this scoping aspect difficult, mainly because they feel unsure about what to collect and how to determine the quality of what is found and read (Chen, Wang & Lee, 2016, p. 50).

14 This number has also been recommended by Aveyard (2010, p. 80).

Suppose your enquiry relates to 'access to justice' involving consumer rights and online shopping. It is possible that your search for materials directs you to a very interesting article about virtual business regulation. In view of your topic, it will be obligatory to evaluate to what extent this piece will assist you in developing your point (Bryman, 2008, p. 100) and understanding the subject (Oliver, 2012, p. 89). In principle, this literature source relates to your topic, but it is up to you – considering the body of the literature, your emphasis, your goals – to decide whether it contributes to your work. No matter whether you choose to keep or discard it, either way, it is crucial that you can demonstrate the reason why it was or was not relevant to your work. Generally, we recommend that you do not go easy on yourself here. You may come across many interesting works, but if those works cannot be expected to contribute to your literature review, discard them from your literature review and save them for later. For instance, if you want to understand how critical legal scholars assess a certain aspect of labor law, you will have to exclude sources that do not refer to this school of thought, even if they discuss that precise issue.

If reducing your list on the basis of the relevance-criterion still leaves you with a lot more than twenty sources, the next thing you can do to downsize it is use the formal criteria we presented above. You may, for instance, find that several of the pieces that are closely related to your review topic are in fact brief informative or opinion pieces produced by non-academics and can therefore (especially if you have enough other sources to rely on) be excluded from your literature review. Textbooks can be removed from your list if there are enough more reflective books and articles to consult. And, if there is an abundance of information that focuses on the tight topic of your literature review, you may even consider leaving out some of the older works, especially those that are discussed in more recent works you do plan to include in your literature review.

According to Denney and Tewksbury (2015, p. 229), "[a]lthough it is important to include a mixture of classic and more recent studies in the literature review, there also exists a balance that will vary from topic-to-topic. The best framework to follow when deciding what/what not to include in the classic studies is to only include the cornerstone research of the topic".

We have said it before and we will say it again: evaluating the sources which will form your literature review is an ongoing process throughout the research trajectory. Even at this point, what may seem to be a 'key' publication for your literature review may later on prove not to be as useful as you thought. Or, the opposite, what you dismissed as irrelevant or not of sufficient quality on the basis of formal criteria, may in the end appear to be more appropriate than first anticipated.

5.4   Reaching a quality judgment on your 'key' sources

Now that you are down to, say, twenty sources that are 'key' to your review topic, you will have to become aware of the strengths and limitations of each of those works. Only then, will you be able to determine how to discuss those sources properly in your final literature review and what weight to attribute to each of these sources. In principle, you should never cite an author without some analysis of the quality of the contribution this author makes to your debate.[15] In this paragraph, we will set out several suggestions on how to evaluate your 'key' sources systematically.

Becoming familiar with your 'key' sources

To be able to make any statement about the strengths and limitations of a particular source, you should always first invest in becoming familiar with both that source *and* its place among the other sources on your topic. The only way to do so is to carefully read, reread, and reread again all of your 'key' sources. Indeed, a significant portion of the time dedicated to the construction of your literature review will be consumed by reading. When you have just started reading, it is quite normal to feel completely swamped by the amount of information that you have to absorb. Do not panic though. You *will* eventually be able to make sense of all that information, as long as you take your time to get acquainted with all of it.

Being familiar with a particular source does not just mean that you can reproduce its findings, but rather that you grasp the author's assumptions, critiques, theoretical influences, methods, discussions with other authors in the field, et cetera (Aveyard, 2010, p. 97; Bryman, 2008, p. 98). As a rule of thumb, we recommend that you do not stop reading your 'key' sources until you can summarize what is going on with respect to all of these matters in each of them. You should fully understand what the author meant with the whole paper and in each particular section. Moreover, you must pay attention to the intertextualities and 'partnerships' (do the authors have a dialogue with each other? On what aspects is there consensus and on what aspects non-consensus? How do they interpret each other's work?). It is important to consider the merits of each individual report, but also to remember that each single piece of research contributes just part of the bigger picture and should thus not be viewed in isolation (Aveyard, 2010, p. 13).

Criticizing your 'key' sources

Once you have become familiar with your literature, the next step is to appraise the literature that you have on a deeper, methodological, level. It is time to take a more critical and skeptical attitude towards your 'key' sources (Oliver, 2012, p. 79). Be aware though that criticism means something other than bitterness or envy! Criticizing certainly does not mean that you have to point out every single, minor flaw in the critiqued object (compare Aveyard, 2010, pp. 93-94). Rather, critical appraisal entails weighing up those flaws in order to make an informed judgment (Garrad, 2011, p. 132). Critiquing is completely compatible with deference to

---

15 Perhaps unless you are summarizing well-known arguments at the beginning of your literature review (see Aveyard, 2010, p. 93, arguing that you can cite an author without analyzing her contribution to the debate when "you are summarizing well-known arguments at the beginning of your literature review, or summarizing arguments in your discussion").

other people's work, but on the other hand, deference does not equate to blind acceptance of the previous research that has been undertaken.

> According to Aveyard (2010, p. 93) those new to academic writing often fall into one of two categories. The first group accepts any piece of research or other information at face value and so accepts what is written without question. They cite a reference without any statement about the quality or authenticity of the report. When a paper is, in particular, published in a reputable journal, such as the *Harvard Law Journal*, they accept it to be above critique and do not attempt any structured appraisal of the paper. The second group interprets the term 'critical appraisal' to mean that they must criticize and find fault in everything they read. They feel that unless they demonstrably tear to pieces what they find, they have not done their job. While it is possible to find fault with every piece of research, it needs to be remembered that no research is perfect.

You need to question how sound a source is. For instance, if an author claims to employ originalism as her approach, evaluate if she is actually applying it. Do not merely accept an author arguing that a legal provision reads like this or like that; question if her reading is precise in light of the related legal principles and other authors' opinions. We recommend that you start by referring to the classification schemes we introduced in *paragraph 3.3* and *paragraph 3.4*. Once you have identified the type of literature you have, you can then look more closely at it. To do so, we recommend that you use the substantive criteria we proposed in *paragraph 5.2*. These will allow you to reach a motivated quality judgment.

> It is important to note that using the quality criteria we proposed does not help you if you do not understand the fundamental principles of the research design (comparative, law and economics, doctrinal) of the study you are critiquing. It is therefore important to become familiar with the basic research methods of the research papers you have identified. If you have identified comparative law studies, become familiar with comparative law by reading *on* comparative law methods. Take this seriously, but keep in mind that for the purpose of appraising your 'key' sources you are not expected to develop an in-depth understanding of every research approach in the way that you would need to if you were pursuing such a design yourself.

5.5   Note-taking and the distillation of relevant information

We recommend that you take detailed notes about how you refine your literature (*paragraph 5.3*) and reach your quality judgment (*paragraph 5.4*), and that you start distilling and organizing the information you come across in the process. Quite often, students just underline and write small observations in the margins of the papers they read, so they can fall back on these annotations later on. After hundreds of thousands of words though, highlights and underlines may turn into a jumble of scribbled papers. Of course, you can highlight and scribble in the literature sources, as a matter of fact, you should even do so. Our goal here is to emphasize that you should not *only* do this.

Instead of summarizing all of the findings of the source you are appraising, we think it is best if you only distil the information you are going to need for your literature review. The publication you scrutinize may deal with many different aspects that are not necessarily all of interest to your enquiry. Summarizing the findings of the whole publication would then not only be unnecessary, but may also tempt you to incorporate the superfluous information from your appraisal file in your literature review.

Furthermore, we remark that you will probably have to revisit the literature as you progress. You might start noticing aspects that were not apparent in the first instance. In research on the interpretation of contracts, you might not have paid much attention to a reference to 'good-faith' when you read a source for the first time. When it appears again further on in the material, you may want to skip back to the articles you have read before in order to make sure that you did not miss it or misinterpret it. Or perhaps you feel that you did not fully understand an author's idea, so you need to check it once more. Sometimes, it is good just to go over a text again with a more learned spirit, because you may come to understand it differently than earlier on in your research.[16]

Create one or more note file(s)

The first step in taking good notes is to have a separate space to register them. It can be an electronic file (per source, or for all the sources together), specific software, or a notebook. When you finish reading the texts, it will be easier to look at the big picture, keywords, commonalities and divergences in one or a couple of concise documents than in the scattered pages of the sources, each with different layouts, and writing styles (Garrad, 2011, p. 107). Taking note of all the aspects mentioned in *paragraph 5.2 and* at the same time distilling relevant information from your sources may seem hard to accomplish, but it is not impossible if you have an organized, ordered way of doing so. We believe a template can be of help here. We recommend you create a table to this end (per source, or one that allows the archiving of information about all of your 'key' sources in one single table).

The latter structure feeds from Garrad (2011), proposing a 'matrix method'. According to this method, the reviewer must create a matrix (spreadsheet or table) with columns displaying topics used to abstract the document (year of publication, author, methods, sample size) and rows where the sources will be detailed. The matrix must observe chronological order to allow the researcher to analyze the evolution of the pieces of research in the area.

What to take notes about?

The next question is how best to label the columns and tables of your file. We advise you to create at least several sections in your note file(s) (see *table 5.1*). In

---

16   According to Wisker (2015, p. 68), as each element of the research is layered in, there should be a new, deeper, more selective understanding of previous reading and newly discovered essential literature to both theorize and situate the work.

the first section (*1*), deal with the formal information of the source. What is the title and date of publication, who is the author (also provide some information on the author's background), in which journal is it published, and are there any bibliometrics available? In the next section (*2*), insert your notes about the precise relevance of the source for your review topic. Hereafter, you could create several sections where you can input the information you come across that may be useful for the construction of your literature review later on. We recommend that you create a section in which you can note information about (*3*) the backgrounds of your review topic, (*4*) the possible significance of doing research related to your topic, (*5*) your project's context, (*6*) definitions of concepts, (*7*) the question asked and the methods and techniques developed to answer it, and (*8*) the findings/results.

Table 5.1   Example of a note file for a single source

Note file

Section	Passages / summaries	Provisional codes
Title & publication date	A Comparison of US and UK Asbestos Liability (2003)	
Author	Wyckoff and McBride	
Journal	Environmental Claims Law Journal (B-status)	
Bibliometric data	Accessed 6 times (Hein Online)	
Relevance		
Background	"Since 1982, RAND has conducted comprehensive examinations of the impact of asbestos liabilities on the U.S. workforce, economy, and court system (RAND, 2002)" (p. 418)	
Potential significance		
Project context		
Definition of concepts	Asbestos: "any of several minerals (such as chrysotile) that readily separate into long flexible fibers, that cause asbestosis and have been implicated as causes of certain cancers, and that have been used especially formerly as fireproof insulating materials" (p. 423)	

Note file

Section	Passages / summaries	Provisional codes
Methods and techniques	Comparative law, comparing UK and US, functional method	
Findings/results	"The preceding review suggests that the U.K.'s current asbestos liability situation may be similar to what the U.S. experienced in the mid-1980s" (p. 424)	
Strengths & limitations	Context was not taken into account when comparing	
Links with other sources		
Thoughts and impressions		

Later on, you will be able, more or less directly, to use the information that relates to these sections for the construction of your literature review. Apart from that, also (*9*) take notes about your quality judgment of a particular source (see *paragraph 5.4*). Add information about the strengths, weaknesses, and (implicit and explicit) limitations regarding either the methods or the conclusions (Bryman, 2008, p. 99).[17] Also (*10*) make notes about the links with other key sources you come across or make yourself.[18] Finally (*11*), write down your own thoughts while reading the sources. As you sharpen your eye to the subject, you will become more critical and develop new analytical perceptions based on what you are reading. Take notes of these thoughts too; they might contain precious insights that can be used when discussing and synthesizing the literature (Oliver, 2012, p. 91).

> Each of these sections or the complete form can, of course, be adjusted in accordance with the topic you are examining. Also, using the template we propose should not hinder you from taking extra notes that do not fit your original fields, but it is a starting point that prevents you from having disconnected notes. If you use (a, modified to your needs, version of) this template while reading the literature, you will, by the end of this phase, have all the key information side by side in one structured and easy to consult document, allowing you to assess the findings.

---

17 For instance, consider whether the author unjustifiably refers to a limited number of authors or has included a one-sided case law selection.

18 *E.g.* do the authors refer to each other? Are there disagreements/agreements among the authors? Are there any gaps or patterns in the literature? What are the mainstream and opposing positions? Which studies or authors are repeatedly cited? And so on.

How to take notes?

You have several options for taking notes: you can copy-paste complete passages, summarize passages, or write down your own interpretation of a passage directly. As the information you put in your final literature review should be credible – in the sense that what others have said was not twisted to fit your own thoughts and needs – we recommend the novice researcher to work with complete passages and comprehensive summaries, rather than (or in combination with) her own interpretations. You probably do not know enough about your topic yet to ensure your interpretation reflects what another author meant.[19] From experience, we know that if you do not do so, you will have to go back numerous times to the original sources as you start doubting whether your notes were correct. Be sure to instantly add the page numbers where the passage you incorporated in your note file can be found, so you do not have to waste time looking for it later on.

5.6   Assign provisional codes to the information

While the process of coding and categorizing is part of the synthesis process (**chapter 6**), we recommend you already start categorizing and coding information at the appraisal stage. That may save you some time when you advance and improve the quality of your literature review, since the more you go over your data and analysis, the more accurate it will become. In *paragraph 6.2* we will provide more information on how to code and categorize your information in a meaningful way.

5.7   Summary and key points

In this chapter, we introduced an appraisal tool that you can use to refine the literature that will comprise your review, weigh up each source and annotate the information it conveys. To critically appraise the literature, you should:

1. apply the relevance-criterion and the formal criteria in order to reduce your initial search results to a researchable size. The former relates to how the source discusses your topic (centrally or marginally) and must be the first criteria you use. If still not sufficient to downsize your sources, you should apply the latter – which refers to non-substantive aspects (*e.g.* how recent a publication is, the reputation of the author and journal, bibliometrics) that will provide an objective account of your selection process;
2. evaluate the quality of the selected sources by getting familiar with and being critical about the sources. The substantive criteria (quality standards that each type of research should meet) will assist you in making an informed judgment about the quality of the sources;

---

19   Chen, Wang & Lee (2016, p. 50) found that empirical studies have revealed that novice researchers do not possess sufficient competency in interpreting findings and key ideas from the literature: "On their own, they are not able to distill higher level meanings from the articles".

3. in a separate file, set up specifically for this purpose, take notes on the formal information about the source (*e.g.* author, date), the background of your topic, the possible relevance to your topic, the definitions and concepts used by the authors, the results and quality of their research, and possible connections with other sources. These notes can take the form of a summary or they can be excerpts you copied-pasted (recommended for novice researchers). You should also take notes of your own thoughts and impressions while reading;

4. assign codes to key information as you read it, but regard them as provisional, as you still need to start the process of synthesizing the information (**chapter 6**).

6 Synthesize, discuss and present your findings

6.1 Introduction

At this point, you already know why you need to do a literature review (**chapter 2**), the literature that is important considering your topic (**chapter 3**), how to gather the body of literature you need (**chapter 4**), and how to select and read the sources that are key to your project both efficiently and critically (**chapter 5**). You now enter the final stage of your literature review. It is time to synthesize the sources that are key to your review topic and to present your findings. The notes you took and categories and codes you developed in the appraisal stage (see *paragraph 5.5* and *paragraph 5.6*) are the starting point of this process. They will enable you to bring the different studies together thematically and find new meaning from the whole that cannot be reached by reading only one study individually (Aveyard, 2010, p. 24; Knopf, 2006, p. 127).

There are two contrary forces underpinning the process of synthesis (Samuel, 2014, p. 27). On the one hand, you will have to show what others have done – map the 'state of the art' – to highlight the importance of your work in the face of the body of knowledge (*paragraph 6.2*). Here, you should not limit yourself to merely summarizing the publications of others. You are expected to explain the differences and point out the reasons for divergence (*e.g.* the methods were different), as well as to identify similarities that may not have been apparent to the authors of the individual pieces. On the other hand, you will have to demonstrate that the picture is not yet complete and there is still room for your research (*paragraph 6.3*). Depending on the context in which you did your systematic literature review, you may subsequently also have to phrase one or more research questions that flow logically from your review (*paragraph 6.4*).

In our experience, instructors or supervisors generally do not ask you to write your preliminary literature review down as a separate product. Rather, they expect you to directly incorporate the findings from your review in an introductory paragraph or chapter of your bigger research project. In order not to leave the issue of how to present your findings untouched, we will, in the conclusion of this chapter, provide you with some general guidelines that you may take into consideration when doing either of those (*paragraph 6.5* and *paragraph 6.6*).

6.2   Identifying the state of the art

The final stage of your literature review starts with synthesizing all the information you gathered. Or, in other words, the identification of the 'state of the art' (the existing body of knowledge, with attention paid to the latest developments and debates) with respect to your review topic. We remind you that this process is *not* just a matter of merely consecutively summarizing each of the publications you classified as 'key'. Rather, you should try to *bring* all of these studies *together* in a comprehensive way (see *paragraph 2.7*). Your goal is to "produce a new and integrative interpretation of findings that is more substantive than those resulting from individual investigation" (Finfgeld, 2003, p. 894). You are advised to include everything that is relevant to your review, but to acknowledge the limitations (see *paragraph 5.4*) of the literature and hence the weight or impact that the literature has in addressing your review topic.

Doing so might seem like a daunting task. Empirical research (Wisker 2015, pp. 69-70) among students who have completed a literature review, reported that they experienced regular moments of blockage ('I hit a brick wall', 'I stopped moving'), but also a breakthrough ('a light went on', 'the fog cleared', 'a jigsaw piece coming together'). While you may reach your personal breakthrough by simply reading and re-reading the collected materials, more technical procedures of coding and categorizing exist that you may want to follow here. For the novice researcher, we recommend the latter over the former.[1] Following a technical procedure not only enables you to tackle the baffling challenge you stand before in a step-by-step manner (and thus make this task manageable – although still hard –) but also enhances your chances of meeting the requirements of an outstanding review.[2] While there are many technical approaches that can be employed (as is evidenced by the overwhelming literature on how to integrate research findings in other academic disciplines[3]), we present just one – simplified – approach (the basics) to coding and categorizing your information which we consider to be accessible and helpful to the novice legal researcher (mainly based on Aveyard, 2010, pp. 128-133).

---

[1]   More experienced researchers may more easily be able to classify information in a meaningful way just from reading it. Codes and categories take shape in the mind of the researcher. For the novice researcher, we believe such an approach to be too risky.

[2]   See Aveyard (2010, p. 124) stating that "[i]n other disciplines, some researchers have argued that it is not appropriate to attempt to bring together the results of research studies at all; to do so is to strip the work of the depth and insight that it gives and that, as a consequence, all (...) research should stand alone rather than be combined. Yet, if (...) research is considered to be generalizable, then the results have to be viewed in relation to others"(citations omitted).

[3]   In all instances, there is a (more or less explicit) element of coding and categorizing involved in this process, to which whole books and book chapters have been dedicated (for instance Charmaz, 2006; Glaser & Strauss, 2006; Lincoln & Guba, 1985). While there are many more materials that deal with coding, we found those particularly helpful when we were ourselves involved in the coding process.

To give you an idea about what we mean with an 'integrative interpretation' of the collected materials, a highly simplified example might be useful. Suppose you are interested in a meta-legal topic, for instance the quality standards that apply to the use of sources in traditional legal scholarship.[4] You should prevent your literature review from ending up something like this: 'Author X finds it necessary to study how legal scholars make use of their sources because globalization has presented many challenges to the contemporary legal researcher. Author X proposes to do this by an empirical investigation among legal scholars, as that might reveal the true complexity of the challenges that legal scholars encounter in daily research practice. Author Y emphasizes the importance of researching the way in which legal scholars employ their research materials since digitalization and Europeanization have resulted in a situation in which more materials than ever before are now accessible, making it extremely difficult to make sense of all that information'. Rather, you should look for something like: 'In the literature, several reasons can be found for pursuing an empirical investigation into the quality standards that apply to the use of sources when legal scholars are involved in 'traditional legal scholarship'. Author X and author Y observe that the globalization of legal scholarship and the law itself has increased the complexity of the source-landscape. Author Y also mentions that the increasing wealth of accessible information as a result of digitalization further justifies an investigation into what can be expected of the legal scholar when pursuing traditional legal research'.

Organizing your information and assigning codes to it

The first step of our approach involves organizing the information you extracted from your sources during the critical appraisal phase and assigning codes to it. If you followed our recommendations in *paragraph 5.5*, the critical appraisal stage has resulted in a table, matrix, or separate file per source that is 'key' to your review topic and holds information that relates to (*1*) the background of your topic, (*2*) the possible significance of doing research into your topic, (*3*) your project's context, (*4*) definitions of concepts, (*5*) the methods and techniques that others employed, and (*6*) the findings/results (see *table 5.1*). Your first task will be an easy one: place the information you previously put in each of these global sections together in separate files.

Once you have done so, it is time to – section-by-section – start assigning codes to all of the information. While part of that information may already have been provided with provisional codes during the appraisal stage (see *paragraph 5.6*), it is now time to start reconsidering these codes and to assign codes to each segment of the information that did not already get a code. According to Charmaz (2006, pp. 47-58), there are a few things to take into consideration when involved in this process of *initial coding*: (*1*) stick closely to the information itself, (*2*) keep your codes simple and precise, (*3*) do not rely (too much) on earlier concepts you know of, and (*4*) try to view your codes as provisional (you will probably have to revise some of them later on). We provide a simplified example (related to the meta-legal project we introduced above) in *table 6.1*.

---

4   One of the projects one of us worked on, see Snel (2017b).

Table 6.1   Example of an initial coding scheme

Coding scheme – section 'Background information'

Quotation or summary of a text	Codes
"Source collection has become more complex as a result of the internet" (author X, p. 11)	Digitalization
"The influence of the European Union, international treaties and the development of globalization of law and legal scholars more generally has made the source-landscape more complex" (author Y, p. 11)	Europeanization
	Internationalization
	Globalization
"ICT-tools (Nvivo) may help in analyzing sources" (author X, p. 15)	Computerization
"Legal scholars do not explicate their methods" (author Z, p. 311)	Non-explication of methods
"Techniques should be mapped empirically" (author Z, p. 122)	Call for methods

When assigning codes, it is important that you use what Glaser and Strauss (1967) call 'constant comparative methods' to establish analytic distinctions. For example, compare an argument, findings, or statement of author X with other arguments, findings, or statements of author X *and* with arguments, findings, or statements of author Y. It is important that you keep in mind that what you see in the information relies in part upon your prior perspectives. Rather than seeing your perspectives as truth, try to see them as representing one view among many. Invoking your own concepts in your codes can lead you to prejudge what is happening and eventually erode the reliability of your review.

Develop categories, and possibly subcategories, and reinforce codes

Subsequently, you should get involved in a more focused, selective phase that uses the most significant or frequent initial codes to sort, synthesize, integrate, and organize all the information you collected (Charmaz, 2006, pp. 57-65). We recommend that you go through your initial codes and see whether (*1*) you still believe them to be correct on second consideration, (*2*) which of them make the most analytic sense for categorizing the information incisively and completely, and (*3*) what interconnections might exist between your codes. Codes that are similar or, as we like to put it, 'similar-but-different' can be grouped together in categories (and perhaps subcategories). Of course, again, the name of a (sub)category should reflect the content of that category. We recommend that, when engaged in this process, you keep the original documents to hand to check the accuracy of the codes you have assigned. Continue this process of assigning each code into a category until all your codes have been assigned and you are left with a small (or smaller) number of categories.[5]

> The codes 'internationalization', 'Europeanization', and 'Globalization' from *table 6.1* may be grouped in a single category that is named 'Globalization' with subcategories 'internationalization' and 'Europeanization'. The codes 'digitalization' and 'computerization' can be put together under the heading 'technological developments'. Finally, the codes 'tradition of non-explication' and 'call for developing methods' form separate categories, as they cannot be grouped together or with any of the other codes and categories we have formed so far. These categories may later form separate (sub)paragraphs when you discuss the background of your review topic in your final literature review.

Comparing and checking your codes and categories

The last step of the approach we propose, is to revisit each category and check at least three things. Firstly, that the name of the category fits all the codes that have been assigned to it.[6] Secondly, that there are no coded sections of results that, on closer analysis, would be better suited to a different category. And thirdly, specify the properties and dimensions of each category by reassembling the information you have fractured during initial coding to give coherence to the emerging analysis (referred to as 'axial coding' by Strauss & Corbin, 1998).[7] At this point, the similarities and differences in the findings of your review will begin to emerge. Look closely at the codes and (sub)categories you have developed and begin to consider how they are linked. As, in our experience, you will find you have further questions with respect to your key publications, it is – again – important to keep the original documents close to hand at this stage. By now, slowly but surely, you should begin to feel more comfortable and confident with the picture that is starting to emerge.[8]

During this process, you might find that you have individual codes or categories that do not support each other (*i.e.* that different, contradictory insights exist within the literature). If this is the case, consider why this may be so. What were the differences in the pieces of research that may account for the different findings? Is one piece of evidence stronger than the other (you may turn to your critical appraisal of the contradictory materials, see *paragraph 5.4*)? Whatever you find, we urge you to document this carefully. Give more weight to research that provides

---

5   There are some tools to assist you in connecting the codes. For one thing, it is helpful to visualize the mapping exercise on a piece of paper, connecting different 'hubs' of codes and categories to each other. There are also software packages that can help you with this task (for example, *NVivo*).

6   As Reitz (1998:625) put it, comparing apples and oranges forces you to create the 'fruit' category. But be aware of not losing sensitivity to nuances.

7   *I.e.* explicate the subcategories and nuances present in the information that belongs to a particular category.

8   Lincoln and Guba (1985, p. 342) describe how this dynamic working back and forth gives the researcher confidence that the development of themes is robust and open to scrutiny.

stronger evidence than to the weaker paper, but explicate that you did this and why you did it. If no explanation is available, present the differing accounts and say that you cannot explain the differences. It is important to describe the differences in results that you find and not to attempt to hide them in order to make your results appear more coherent (Aveyard, 2010, pp. 131-132). If all the information suggests different things, document this and say that you cannot reach firm conclusions from the information you have.

> For example, one small-scale study carried out on a small sample of judicial opinions might demonstrate different results from that obtained in a larger-scale study undertaken with a more representative sample. You would be more likely to give greater weight to the results of the larger study, but do not forget to mention the other study as well (compare the example provided by Epstein & King, 2002, pp. 32-34). If you find that the differences in the results can be explained by the sample sizes used, be sure to mention it in your review!

You can now evaluate whether your findings support or contradict each other. In one word, you will look at the *coherence* of the body of knowledge. According to the literature, there are three possibilities when it comes to intertextual coherence (Bryman, 2008, p. 100; Samuel, 2014, p. 27). The first one (*1*) is the synthesized coherence: you will be able to bring together works that are generally considered unconnected, demonstrating an underlying coherence between them. If your research involves different disciplines, there is a good chance that works pointing in the same direction are scattered (Samuel, 2014, p. 28). and have not been related before. You will be capable of synthesizing them. The second (*2*) is called progressive coherence: you can see how the current consensus was forged over time, *i.e.* how the researchers have been applying shared theoretical frameworks and methods to study the topic, which ends up developing lines of enquiry on the issue (Samuel, 2014, p. 28). Finally, there is (*3*) non-coherence: you will notice that there is considerable disagreement among the authors, so the sources are linked by discord.

6.3   Identifying gaps in the body of knowledge

The next step of your literature review is to identify one or more angles worth being examined by an academic legal research project. Therefore, you should try to find the gaps in the body of knowledge and indicate the expected contribution to this body that you are putting forward. Doing so is pivotal, as only research questions that address these gaps will be considered academically relevant (see *paragraph 2.5*). We remark that the term 'gaps' may be slightly misleading here, as it suggests that if an area has been 'covered' there is no longer a gap. However, it can also be the case that a particular topic has been covered, but that you disagree (for good reasons that you will need to explain) with how it has been covered. Thus, in general, gaps are an account of both the completeness *and* accuracy of the literature sources, considering what is right, wrong, inconclusive, or missing (Knopf, 2006, p. 127). We will discuss the four main types of gaps in more depth to help you on your way: incompleteness, inadequacy, incommensurability, and non-consensus (compare Bryman, 2008, p. 84; Samuel, 2014, p. 29).[9]

Incompleteness

Once you have identified the state of the art, you may realize that some aspects have not (or not yet) been addressed by the legal scholarly community before. Sometimes the sources themselves refer to one or more facets that need more investigation and sometimes you will have to recognize this yourself. Generally, you could say that if your topic is X and you could see during your review that X_1, X_2, and X_4 have been discussed but there are no discussions about X_3 and X_5, this may be a reason to dive deeper into X_3 or X_5. An example might provide further clarification. You may find that there is an abundance of literature relating to the determination of the height of administrative fines, but that relatively little is known about the influence that the financial standing of an offender may have on the determination of the height of a fine. That could be a reason to seize the opportunity to fill this gap. For instance, by starting a project in which you try to identify whether lower courts have actually taken financial standing into account in prior legal disputes or by starting a comparative analysis to see whether other jurisdictions allow (and if so, in what ways) consideration of the financial standing of an offender in the context of administrative fines.

Inadequacy

Apart from encountering a situation where the debate on your review topic is incomplete, you might also find that the existing literature has disregarded approaches or perspectives that seem accurate or that could improve the understanding of the issue. For example, if you look into the civil liability of governmental agencies for damages (partly) caused by insufficient or inadequate supervision and there are no studies tackling this issue from a, say, law and economics perspective (which seems to be one of the adequate ways of understanding this topic), then that might be an interesting angle to pursue in a bigger research project. In this case, it is not that a particular aspect has not been addressed, as in the previous point, but rather that an insight has not been examined through a certain lens. You might ask yourself whether, in view of the body of research you encountered, authors seem to repeat the same assumptions and use the same theoretical lens, and if so, why the subject has not been assessed from another angle. After all, academic originality is also about adding a new perspective to settled themes (compare Guetzkow, Lamont, & Mallard, 2004; Siems, 2008)!

---

9   Gaps are facets of the literature that can be either filled or tackled from another point of view. The latter will eventually touch upon points that seem sedimented but require a new light. The literature review will highlight blind spots in areas that were deemed to be consensual, which could be used to propose research that might defy conventional wisdom (Knopf, 2006, p. 130).

Incommensurability

Another gap you might be able to identify, relates to the situation in which the reviewer argues that the existing literature is 'wrong, misguided, or incorrect' (Golden-Biddle & Locke, 1993). You might find for instance, on the basis of your literature review, that while there are several scholars who have mapped lower court case law with regard to a particular doctrine, they have not done so comprehensively (on the basis of too small a sample, for example). That then may be a reason to focus your bigger research project on a comprehensive analysis of the lower court case law with regard to that doctrine. While many other situations are imaginable, what characterizes focusing your literature review on these types of gaps is that you claim to have "an alternative perspective that is superior to the literature as it stands" (Bryman, 2008, p. 84).[10]

Non-consensus

A final type of gap may be identified if you encounter a source that does not fit the overall debate or if you spot the existence of an unsettled debate with regard to your review topic (Aveyard, 2010, p. 7; Oliver, 2012, p. 77). Instead of just dismissing a source that seems to represent an isolated approach to or interpretation of your review topic, you might want to evaluate whether this is not a thread worth pursuing in more depth. It might be "an appropriate, creative, or necessary diversion from the mainstream of research" (Garrad, 2011, p. 133) that will help reshape traditional understanding. If you come across unsettled debates – *i.e.* differences of opinion among authors who have contributed to the field – this might also be a reason to research the debated issue further. Can the difference of opinion be explained? And is there a way of looking at the matter from another angle that might contribute to solving the debated issue (even if only partly)?

> Be aware though that it might also be the case that arguments and perspectives on a particular topic have been exhausted. In the Netherlands (and many other countries), the debate on the introduction of constitutional review serves as an example. Everything there is to say about the introduction of constitutional review has by now been said.

6.4   Developing your research question

At the beginning of this book, we stated that our focus was to provide guidance on how to undertake a literature review that is part of a bigger project. Here, the literature review serves to assist you in embedding your topic in the body of knowledge and helps you identify a path to follow. Or, in other words, to find a research question. The subsequent question then is: what constitutes a 'good' research question?

---

10   Samuel (2014, p. 29) argues that, although it is possible to hold such claims, they are rather complicated in legal scholarship because the assertions are not falsifiable. He recommends that the reviewer does not simply dismiss an author's claim because another argued it was wrong, but that she registers that there is an ongoing debate.

We have to remind you that the answer to this question falls outside the scope of this book. While we will thus not be presenting an in-depth consideration of this particular research activity, we do want to make a few important remarks here. Firstly, we believe your research question should generally be focused on *one* of the gaps you have identified, not on multiple gaps or all of them. By phrasing your research question, you will probably thus further delineate the topic of your bigger research project (see *figure 3.1*). That delineation may in turn also have consequences for the findings of your literature review that you should incorporate into your bigger project (*i.e.* when you are answering your research question and writing your work). Perhaps, most of what you found in your literature review relates to other gaps than the one you are interested in, so that it has become redundant for your bigger project and should therefore be barred from it (see *paragraph 6.5* for some more elaboration).

> For the question of what constitutes a 'good' research question, we confine ourselves to referring to the work of others. Oost's dissertation (1999) is of importance here in that is completely devoted to providing an overview of the quality standards a research question should meet: substantive embodiment, significance and originality, precision, methodical functionality, consistency, and exposition (we already discussed these in *paragraph 2.5*). We also refer to the works of Kestemont (2015), Siems (2008), and Curry-Sumner, Kirsten, Van der Linden-Smith, and Tigchelaar (2010) which contain some general information on what constitutes a 'good' academic research question and provide several examples that may inspire you. Apart from these more general works on phrasing your research question, we however also want to emphasize the importance of considering how other legal scholars operating in the field of your review topic have formulated their questions. That will give you an idea of how academia works in your specific field (compare Bryman, 2008, p. 90).

Whatever research question you phrase, be aware of the fact that an important aspect of any research question is that it is not only connected to the theory but also that this connection is *demonstrated explicitly* (Bryman, 2008, p. 90). The literature review will point to the direction of your research question, but it is important that you make this link clear, displaying the problem under investigation, its relation to theory and how you are going to assess it. The literature review thus assists you not only in finding your research question, but also in justifying its importance.

6.5   Presenting your findings

Now that you have undertaken all the work required to complete your literature review, you have one important task left. That is to present your review in a way that reflects the hard work you have done. What exactly the best way of presenting your findings is depends on the context in which your literature review is constructed. Does your supervisor expect you to present your literature as a separate product, or to directly incorporate the findings of your review in a first paragraph or chapter that is part of your bigger research project? If the former is the case, does she then want you to conclude your literature review by phrasing a particular research question that is worth answering (and that in turn partly determines the information that can be left out of your review) or are you expected to end your review with the identification of one or more gaps you may jump into later on?

> Be aware that writing up your literature review comprehensively cannot be done in one try. It has often been emphasized that a good literature review is most likely a product of frequent, iterative re-writing (see for instance, Wisker, 2015, p. 64).

Constructing an introductory chapter on the basis of your review

If your supervisor expects you to directly transfer your literature review into a first chapter or paragraph, there is probably a lot of information that you have gathered during the review process that you can leave out. Center the information you present on your research question. What information does the reader *need* to know to understand the backdrop against which this question was composed? What information does the reader *need* to know to be convinced about the significance and originality of this question? And so on. Do not take it easy on yourself here. In our experience, there is a natural inclination to include excessive information in an introductory paragraph or chapter. While understandable – you have done so much preliminary research and you want to demonstrate it – adding in everything will usually make your work lengthy, all-over-the-place, difficult to read, and therefore, ultimately, of lesser quality.

Presenting your literature review as a separate product

If you will have to (or want to) present your literature review as a separate product, you can include more information. However, you should also be ready to filter out some of the identified themes or literature because they are not crucially important to your final focus. Some students attempt to use all the literature sources they went through in their review. This should definitely not be an aim in itself. It would be better to focus on the major topics and discard those themes and sources that are only partially or marginally relevant to the gap(s) you are going to elaborate. Constantly keep in mind that the function of a literature review is *not* to showcase your knowledge, but rather to identify the state of the art and the gaps in the body of knowledge. If you are going to present your literature review as a separate product, a general structure you may want to follow is provided below (based on Aveyard, 2010, pp. 148-150). Do not get the wrong impression though: it may be helpful, even necessary, to make subheadings, depending on the specific characteristics of your research project, within each of the sections we will discuss to give further structure to your writing.

Introduction
As a rule of thumb, you should start with a statement in which you introduce the focus of your literature review. It could be something like, "the issue of judicial review is polarized between two strands, despite their internal nuances". From here, you will explain to your reader what these two main strands are and what the most

disputed ideas between and within each of them are. This statement will provide context to the reader about your main purpose and achievements within the review. Alongside this statement, you can provide a little context about the topic you are examining.

Methods
You will have to clearly document the process you followed in constructing your review. Therefore, we recommend that you include a methods section in your review where you will demonstrate that you undertook a comprehensive and systematic approach in collecting (**chapter 4**), appraising (**chapter 5**), and synthesizing (*paragraph 6.2* and *paragraph 6.3*) the body of academic literature that relates to your review topic. The length of this section will depend on the specifics of your project. Sometimes, it can be a brief mention in a footnote, a more elaborate separate section of your text, and/or a full account in an appendix.

Results

After you have presented an account of the focus of your literature review, you will need to show the bulk of your findings. Here, you may use the categories, subcategories and codes you developed to organize your text. In theory, we can think of at least five ways to organize these categories and subcategories. Note that these are just suggestions though. The characteristics of your review topic will ultimately determine how best to present your results.

1. *Chronological.* Although very common in the health sciences field (see Garrad, 2011), we believe that presenting your review following a chronological structure is generally not suited to legal scholarship. Many of the issues that occupy legal scholars generally return every so often, meaning that a chronological presentation of your findings can lead to a repetition of themes that are better grouped together. However, if there was a consistent progression of the approaches to your topic over time, it could be interesting to present this evolution as it happened. This will especially be the case if your theme involves how legal understanding has changed over time.
2. *Topical.* A topical way of presenting your findings means that you divide your broader topic into several subtopics and discuss those consecutively. Here you group together the categories that you identified during the coding process (*paragraph 6.2*) by their substantive coherence, rather than in chronological order, broadness, actuality, or methodology.
3. *Funnel* or *pyramid.* As you might have noticed when going through the literature yourself, some authors prefer to approach a topic from a broad perspective. They may for instance embed the issue they are looking at in a more philosophical or theoretical discussion. When presenting the findings, you can also go from the broad perspective to the narrow one, funneling down the topic. Or, contrariwise, you can start from the latter and go to the former.
4. *Trends.* This approach is similar to the topical presentation of your findings, but more selective, now focusing on recent or previous trends you discovered in the body of academic literature. Perhaps you identified a tendency among

authors to treat the topic that interests you in a certain way. Or you may have found that three issues stand out from the debate that has been going on in recent years. You may then choose to discuss your findings by focusing on the trend(s) you encountered.

5. *Methodological.* A final approach to presenting your findings is by sorting them on the basis of the methodological approaches employed towards your research topic. *I.e.* first comparative law approaches are discussed together, then doctrinal approaches, then 'law and' approaches, and so on. This structure may for instance be suitable if you are planning to apply a new methodological approach to the topic, so you demonstrate through the literature review why that is appropriate (Denney & Tewksbury, 2013, p. 230).

Denney and Tewksbury (2013, p. 220, 232) advocate a funnel approach in criminal justice research. They state: "First and foremost, literature reviews include a comprehensive overview of a general topic. For example, if there was a study on whether alcohol abuse leads to the tendency to commit violent crimes, then it would need to have an overview of substance abuse issues (not just alcohol abuse) and how such may influence all types of crime. First, the review of this literature should start with the general topic of substance abuse and how it influences committing all types of crime. Then, it should discuss different types of substance abuse (*i.e.* prescription drug abuse, alcohol abuse, etc.). Next, it would need to discuss the influence of substance abuse on general types of crime (*i.e.* petty theft, property crimes, violent crimes, etc.). Finally, it would need to focus on the primary subtopics of alcohol abuse (*i.e.* psychological affects, behavioral affects, etc.) and its direct influence on committing violent crimes. In essence, the literature review goes from a broad overview to a specific focus by using subtopics of the general research question to guide the focus to a specific research question that the author wants to address".

Conclusions

If you have followed the steps identified above, you should arrive at describing the state of the art. However, describing the state of the art is not always the same as identifying it. One can encounter well-written and good literature reviews that fall short on the final and most crucial step of explicitly stating what the state of the art is. Just like any good piece of writing, your literature review therefore needs a concluding section. Here, you conclude the state of the art by summarizing, in a few concise sentences, the general meaning of what your review has found (Aveyard, 2010, p. 143). After summarizing the state of the art, finish the literature review by connecting the findings to what you are going to develop from now on. After all, in academic writings, examiners "look for evidence that the candidate uses the literature to develop an argument, to connect with her findings, or to develop a distinctive stance on the subject" (Bryman, 2008, p. 84), instead of merely listing previous research.

Go beyond the mere stating of opinions and arguments of others

Finally, we want to emphasize some more general remarks we think are important when it comes to writing down your literature review. Firstly, you should not write down opinions, arguments, insights or statements of other authors without at least also explaining the background and/or context thereof. For instance, if you state that author X and Y both think that the current legal regime on when a party is obliged to send a default notice before claiming damages is both complex and unclear, make sure you also explain why author X and Y come to this conclusion. In our experience, novice researchers in particular, tend to forget to go beyond the mere stating of opinions and arguments. Revisiting your appraisal files (**chapter 5**) might be helpful at this point.

> Do not just state that 'Author X claims that ruling Y of the court Z oversteps the boundaries of checks and balances', but also add a short account of the reason why she argues that, her theoretical lens, her method for examining this decision. By adding this information, you are providing your reader with the precision and thoroughness she needs to understand the author's position, the topic, and the debate.
>
> Aveyard (2010, p. 94) provides a hypothetical example: if the only information that is given is 'Smith (2006) argues that university students prefer lectures to tutorials', the reader is unaware of the context from which the author is writing: "[i]t is unclear whether the author is merely citing an opinion or referring to published research or whether the paper is actually the report of empirical findings about students' learning preferences. Further information needs to be given".
>
> Epstein and King (2002, pp. 58-59) have provided a real example from the study of Perrin and others, in which the researchers conducted a survey of policy officers in California with the intention of answering the question 'what are the effects and costs of the exclusionary rule?' which clarifies the point we would like to make here:[11] "[t]o be sure, the authors acknowledge the existing, clearly identifiable body of literature that has bearing on their question. (...) But it is insufficient. Full compliance [with the rules of inference] requires researchers to take into account the lessons of past studies – both their assets and deficits – in their own endeavor. And it was on this dimension that Perrin and his colleagues could have gone much further".

We would like to emphasize that doing this right is no easy task. The empirical study conducted by Wisker (2015, p. 69) on how the literature review is perceived by students, found that "[s]tudents reported early writing struggles, lack of confidence in their own right to speak, tension and compromise with theorists. They realize the theorists and theoretical perspectives should help them focus on their problems and on data when gathered, but they often struggle to understand them, feel humble about interpreting and using them, and can either over-simplify in a cursory fashion or over-complicate".

---

11 Perrin et al. *'If It's Broken, Fix It: Moving Beyond the Exclusionary Rule: A New and Extensive Empirical Study of the Exclusionary Rule and a Call for a Civil Administrative Remedy to Partially Replace the Rule'* (1998).

Separate your voice from the authors'

Also remember to separate your voice from those of the authors you are going to discuss. The reader needs to know what your own ideas are and what information was retrieved from the body of literature. As a rule of thumb, using the first person in literature reviews helps to do so; when you use 'the author' to refer to yourself and to the sources, it can become quite confusing for the reader. Moreover, using this term to refer to sources must be done carefully. Since there are many authors, it will not always be clear to whom you are referring.

Consider the reader when writing up your review

Despite all the efforts structuring your findings in accordance with the themes, while pointing out gaps, contrasting the differences, highlighting the similarities, and filtering the most important works, your text should not read like an instruction manual. Examiners appreciate literature reviews that read pleasantly (see *paragraph 2.8*). According to Boote and Beile (2005, pp. 6-7) "[t]he dirty little secret known by those of us who sit on dissertation committees is that literature reviews are often (if not usually) inadequate, poorly conceptualized and written, and boring". As you should take pleasure in reading the work of others, others should feel the same about yours. Write your review taking the reader into consideration, not just because it is a prerequisite that you want to be done with quickly.

Referencing

When writing a literature review, you attribute claims to others. It is important that your readers can verify these assertions by checking the sources you build on. Enabling this verification of the original source constitutes the *accountability principle* of academic research. To be accountable, it is important to reference the work of others correctly, which implies that (*i*) a reference should be included where the scholar draws from the work of others, (*ii*) the reference should be precise (indicating the exact page(s) or section where the information can be found), and (*iii*) the reference should be correct in the sense that the research materials referred to in fact contain information that supports the interpretation, argument or statement of the researcher.[12]

6.6   Summary and key points

At the final stage of your literature review, you must synthesize and present your findings to the audience. In this task, we assisted you on how to:

---

12 While the importance of precise and correct referencing might sound obvious, it causes quite some problems in research practice, see for instance Harrison and Mashburn (2015).

1. identify the state of the art by attaching cogency to the different sources, which is done through the assignment of codes to the key information in the sources and seeking connections between them (similarities, differences);
2. elaborate the gaps you identified (is the literature incomplete, wrong, tackling the issue from an inadequate perspective, is there an ongoing debate?);
3. phrase a research question that adds to the body of knowledge by linking it to the state of the art you describe and one of the gaps you pointed out;
4. present your findings in accordance with the overall purposes of your project (*i.e.* as a small introductory presentation of the project or as a separate part of the bigger project), but, in any case, provide a context to your reader of the sources you are referring to and make sure that the reader knows which assertions are yours and which are descriptions from the sources.

7 Summary

Throughout this book, we introduced techniques on how to do a systematic literature review in legal scholarship. We believe in its importance for promoting quality in legal scholarship. A call for a systematic approach has been gaining a foothold in legal academic discussions. As you witnessed throughout this book, such an approach requires a lot of work, but it rewards the researcher and the whole of academia with strong pieces that foster the development of legal scholarship and enhance its credibility. Therefore, we firmly believe, systematic literature reviews must be taken seriously by all legal scholars.

Contrary to a disorganized search, appraisal, and review of the literature, a systematic one is replicable and transparent. Due to the procedures it follows, it reduces the researcher's biases and enhances the accountability of the choices and conclusions, minimizing the risk that reviews turn into a haphazard collection of random texts. There is no magic or mystery involved in making your review systematic: it is just a set of techniques.

Indeed, one of the main features of a *systematic* review is that the reviewer has to follow a strict protocol to ensure that the review process undertaken is systematic. This process consists of using explicit and rigorous methods to determine the literature that will be relevant to your literature review (**chapter 3**) and to identify (**chapter 4**), critically appraise (**chapter 5**), and synthesize, discuss and present (**chapter 6**) relevant studies on a particular topic. In this book, we presented what each of these steps entails, as well as why and how to undertake them. If you follow these procedures, you are likely to gain insights and perspectives that you would not have if you went through the literature unsystematically.

Once you have made your decisions about the sources you will need to review, collected them in a structured manner, read them thoroughly and carefully, analyzed their content and were capable of seeing the whole picture they form, you are likely to have found your research question. Not only that, you can argue and demonstrate its significance in the face of the experts' discussions. However, by identifying a relevant research question you only start to give shape to your project. From now on, you will still need to draw other lines, refine the contours and paint the whole the picture. There is still a lot of work ahead of you! But, after undertaking a systematic literature review, you can rest assured that you are on the right track in your enterprise and, by the end, will be able to contribute to the state of the art.

References

Alvesson, M., & Sandberg, J. (2011). Generating research questions through problematization. *Academy of Management Review, 36*(2), 247-271.

Aveyard, H. (2010). *Doing a Literature Review in Health and Social Care: A Practical Guide*. Berkshire: Open University Press.

Barbour, R. S. (2001). Checklist for improving rigour in qualitative research: a case of the tail wagging the dog? *British Medical Journal, 322*(7294), 1115-1117.

Barroso, J., Gollop, C. J., Sandelowski, M., Meynell, J., Pearce, P. F., & Collins, L. J. (2003). The challenges of searching for and retrieving qualitative studies. *Western Journal of Nursing Research, 25*(2), 153-178.

Barry, C. (1997). Information Skills for an Electronic World: Training Doctoral Research Students. *Journal of Information Science, 23*(3), 225-238.

Bartie, S. (2009). The Impact of Legal Meta-Scholarship: Love Thy Navel. *Griffith Law Review, 18*(3), 727-751.

Bartie, S. (2010). The lingering core of legal scholarship. *Legal Studies, 30*(3), 345-369.

Bast, C. M., & Pyle, R. C. (2001). Legal Research in the Computer Age: A Paradigm Shift? *Law Library Journal, 93(2)*, 285-302.

Baude, W., Chilton, A. S., & Malani, A. (2017). Making Doctrinal Work More Rigorous: Lessons from Systematic Reviews. *University of Chicago Law Review, 84*(1), 37-58.

Berring, R. (1997). Chaos, Cyberspace and Tradition: Legal Information Transmogrified. *Berkeley Technological Law Journal, 12*(1), 189-212.

Bodig, M. (2011). *Doctrinal Knowledge, Legal Doctrines and Legal Doctrinal Scholarship*. Retrieved from <http://papers.ssrn.com/sol3/papers.cfm?abstract_id=1921305>

Boote, D. N., & Beile, P. M. (2005). Scholars before researchers: On the centrality of the dissertation literature review in research preparation. *Educational Researcher, 34*(6), 3-15.

Bruce, C. S. (1994). Research students' Early experiences of the Dissertation Literature Review. *Studies in Higher Education, 19*(2), 217-229.

Bryman, A. (2008). *Social Research Methods* (Vol. 3). Oxford: Oxford University Press.

Bunge, M. A. (1967). *Scientific Research I. The search for system*. Dordrecht: Reidel.

Cahillane, L., & Schweppe, J. (2016). *Legal Reserch Methods. Principles and Practicalities*: Clarus Press.

Charmaz, K. (2006). *Constructing Grounded Theory. A Practical Guide Through Qualitative Analysis*. Thousand Oaks: C.A. Sage.

Chen, D.-T., Wang, Y.-M., & Lee, W. C. (2016). Challenges confronting beginning researchers in conducting literature reviews. *Studies in Continuing Education, 38*(1), 47-60.

Clinch, P. (2001). *Using a Law Library: A Student's Guide to Research Skills*. Oxford: Blackwell.

Clinch, P., & Mullan, J. (2010). *Legal research: a practitioner's handbook*. London: Wildy, Simmonds & Hill.

Cohen, M. L., & Olson, K. C. (2007). *Legal research in a nutshell*. St. Paul: Thomson/West.

Cook, T. D., & Campbell, D. T. (1979). *Causi-experimentation: Design and analysis issues for field settings*. Chicago: Rand McNally.

Cooper, H. (1998). *Synthesizing research: a guide for literature reviews*. Thousand Oaks: Sage Publications.

Curry-Sumner, I., Kirsten, F., Van der Linden-Smith, T., & Tigchelaar, J. (2010). *Onderzoeksvaardigheden: instructie voor juristen*. Nijmegen: Ars Aequi Libri.

Dannemann, G. (2006). Comparative Law: Study of Similarities and Differences. In M. Reimann & R. Zimmermann (Eds.), *The Oxford Handbook of Comparative Law* (pp. 383-419). Oxford: Oxford University Press.

Davidson, S. (2010). Way Beyond Legal Research: Understanding the Research Habits of Legal Scholars. *Law Librarian Journal, 102*(4), 561-579.

Denney, A. S., & Tewksbury, R. (2013). How To Write a Literature Review. *Journal of Criminal Justice Education, 24*(2), 218-234.

Dobinson, I., & Johns, F. (2007). Qualitative Legal Research in M. McConville & W. H. Chui (Eds.), *Research methods for law* (pp. 16-45). Edinburgh: Edinburgh University Press.

Drake, A. M. (2016). The Need for Experiental Legal Research Education. *Law Library Journal, 108*(4), 511-535.

Epstein, L., & King, G. (2002). The Rules of Inference. *University of Chicago Law Review, 69*(1), 1-134.

Evans, D. (2002). Database searches for qualitative research. *Journal of the Medical Library Association, 90*(3), 290-293.

Fajans, E., & Falk, M. R. (2011). *Scholarly Writing for Law Students: Seminar Papers, Law Review Notes and Law Review Competition Papers* (4 ed.). Eagan: West Publishing Company.

Finch, E., & Fafinski, S. (2015). *Legal Skills* (5th ed.). Oxford: Oxford University Press.

Finfgeld, D. L. (2003). Metasynthesis: the state of the art so far. *Qualitative Health Research, 13*(7), 893-904.

Fink, A. (2010). *Conducting research literature review: from the internet to paper*. London: Sage.

Fisher, E., Lange, B., Scotford, E., & Carlarne, C. (2009). Maturity and Methodology: Starting a Debate about Environmental Law Scholarship. *Journal of Enviironmental Law, 21*(2), 213-250.

Frankenberg. (2006). How to Do Projects with Comparative Law - Notes of an Expedition to the Common Core. *Global Jurist, 6*(2), 1-30.

Garrad, J. (2011). *Health Sciences Literature Review Made Easy: The Matrix Method* (Vol. 3): Jones & Barlett Learning.

Germain, C. M. (2007). Legal Information Management in a Global and Digital Age: Revolution and Tradition. *International Journal of Legal Information, 35*(1), 134-163.

Glaser, B., & Strauss, A. L. (1967). *The Discovery of Grounded Theory*. Hawthorne, N.Y.: Aldine Publishing Company.

Glaser, B., & Strauss, A. L. (2006). *The Discovery of Grounded Theory: Strategies for Qualitative Research*. New York: Aldine de Gruyter.

Golden-Biddle, K., & Locke, K. D. (1993). Appealing Work: An Investigation of How Ethnographic Texts Convince. *Organization Science, 4*(4), 595-616.

Green, R., & Macauley, P. (2007). Doctoral students' engagement with information: An American-Australian perspective. *Protal: Libraries and the Academy, 7*(3), 317-332.

Greenberg, S. N. (2007). Legal Research Training: Preparing Students for a Rapidly Changing Research Environment. *Legal Writing: Journal of Legal Writing Institution, 13*, 241.

Greenhalgh, T., & Peacock, R. (2005). Effectiveness and Efficiency of search methods in systematic reviews of complex evidence: audit of primary sources. *British Medical Journal, 331*(7524), 1064-1065.

Greenhalgh, T. (2010). *How to Read a Paper*. London: Wiley-Blackwell.

Guetzkow, J., Lamont, M., & Mallard, G. (2004). What is Originality in the Social Sciences and the Humanities? *American Sociological Review, 69*(2), 190-212.

Handler, P. (2013). Legal History. In D. Watkins & M. Burton (Eds.), *Research Methods in Law* (pp. 85-99). London / New York: Routledge.

Hanson, S. (2016). *Learning Legal Skills and Reasoning*. Milton Park & New York: Routledge.

Harrison, J. L., & Mashburn, A. R. (2015). *Citations, Justifications, and the Troubled State of Legal Scholarship: An Empirical Study*. University of Florida Levin College of Law Legal Studies Research Paper Series Paper.

Hart, C. (2001). *Doing a literature search: a comprehensive guide for the social sciences*. London: Sage Publications.

Hillway, T. (1969). *Handbook for Educational Research. A guide to Methods and Materials*. Boston: Houghton Mifflin Company.

Hirschl, R. (2005). The Question of Case Selection in Comparative Constitutional Law. *American Journal of Comparative Law, 53*(1), 125-156.

Holbrook, A., Bourke, S., Fairburn, H., & Lovat, T. (2007). Examiner Comment on the Literature Review in Ph.D. Theses. *Studies in Higher Education, 32*(3), 337-356.

Hondius, E. (2007). De scriptie. *Ars Aequi, 56*(10), 793-794.

Hoogendam, A. F. H., Robbee, P. F., & Overbeke, A. J. (2008). Analysis of queries sent to PubMed at the point of care: observation of search behaviour in a medical teaching hospital. *BMC Med Inform Decis Mak, 8*(42), 1-10.

Husa, J. (2006). Methodology of comparative law today: From paradoxes to flexibility. *Revue internationale de droit compare: revue trimestrielle publiee avec le con-*

cours du CNRS et sous les auspices du Centre Francais de Droit Compare, (4), 1095-1117.

Hutchinson, T. (2010). Researching and writing in law. Sydney: Lawbook Co.

Hutchinson, T. (2013). Doctrinal research. Researching the jury. In D. Watkins & M. Burton (Eds.), *Research Methods in Law* (pp. 7-33). London / New York: Routledge.

Hutchinson, T., & Cuffe, N. (2003). Encouraging Student Research Project Success. *Australian Law Librarian, 11*(4), 341-353.

Ibbetson, D. (2003). What is Legal History a History of? In A. Lewis & M. Lobban (Eds.), *Law and History* (pp. 33-40). Oxford: Oxford University Press.

Katrak, P., Bialocerkowski, A. E., Massy-Westropp, N., Kumar, S., & Grimmer, K. A. (2004). A systematic review of the content of critical appraisal tools. *BMC Medical Research Methodology, 4*(22), 22-33.

Kestemont, L. (2015). A Meta-Methodological Study of Dutch and Belgian PhDs in Social Security Law: Devising a Typology of Research Objectives as a Supporting Tool. *European Journal on Social Security, 17*(3), 361-384.

Kestemont, L. (2016). *Naar een rechtswetenschappelijke methodeleer. Een expliciet methodologisch kader voor rechtswetenschappelijk onderzoek in het socialezekerheidsrecht.*

Knopf, J. W. (2006). Doing a Literature Review. *Political Science and Politics, 39*(1), 127-132.

Korobkin, R. (1999). Ranking Journals: Some Thoughts on Theory and Methodology. *Florida State University Law Review, 26*(4), 851-874.

Korobkin, R. (2002). Empirical Scholarship in Contract Law. Possibilities and Pitfalls. *University of Illinois Law Review, 2002*(4), 1033-1066.

Lagerwaard, H., & Mul, J. (1982). *Scripties onderzocht. Een analyse van de kwaliteit van doctoraalscripties in de culturele antropologie, de politicologie en de sociologie en de tijd, die het schrijven ervan kost.* Leiden: Rijksuniversiteit Leiden.

Lesaffer, R. C. H. (2011). Law and History: Law Between Past and Present. In B. M. J. v. Klink & H. S. Taekema (Eds.), *Law and method: interdiciplinary research into law.* (pp. 133-152). Tübingen: Mohr Siebeck.

Levitt, C. A., & Rosch, M. E. (2010). *Google for lawyers: essential search tips and productivity tools.* Chicago: American Bar Association, Law Practice Management Section.

Lincoln, Y. S., & Guba, E. G. (1985). *Naturalistic Inquiry.* Newbury Park: CA: Sage.

Lovitts, B. E. (2007). *Making the Implicit Explicit: Creating Performace Expectations for the Dissertation.* Sterling: Stylus.

Maier, H. R. (2013). What constitutes a good literature review and why does its quality matter? *Environmental Modelling & Software, 43*, 3-4.

Mart, S. N. (2010). The Relevance of Results Generated by Human Indexing and Computer Algorithms: A Study of West's Headnotes and Key Numbers and LexisNexis's Headnotes and Topics. *Law Library Journal, 102*(2), 221-249.

McCrudden, C. (2006). Legal Research and the Social Sciences. *Law Quarterly Review, 122*(4), 632-650.

Meeker, H. (1996). Stalking the Golden Topic: A Guide to Locating and Selecting Topics for Legal Research Papers. *Utah Law Review, 1996*(3), 917-986.

Mersky, R., & Dunn, D. (2002). Fundamentals of Legal Research. New York: West Group.

Montori, V. M., Wilczynski, N. L., Morgan, D., & Haynes, R. B. (2004). Optimal search strategies for retrieving systematic reviews from medline: an analytical survey. *British Medical Journal, 330*(7482), 1-6.

Morse, J. M. (1999). Qualitative generalizability. *Qualitative Health Research, 9*(1), 5-6.

Neacsu, E. (2007). *Google, Legal Citations, and Electronic Fickleness: Legal Scholarship in the Digital Environment.* Retrieved from <http://ssrn.com/abstract=991190>.

Nelson, W. (1982). Standards of Criticism. *Texas Law Review, 60*(3), 447-494.

Oliver, P. (2012). *Succeeding with your Literature Review. A Handbook for Students.* Berkshire: Open University Press.

Oost, H. (1999). *De formele kwaliteit van probleemstellingen in dissertaties.* Utrecht: W.C.C.

Osborne, C. L. (2012). *A Methodical Approach to Legal Research: The Legal Research Plan, an Essential Tool for Today's Law Student and New Attorney.* Washington & Lee Public Legal Studies Research Paper Series. Washington and Lee University School of Law. Lexington.

Osborne, C. L. (2016). The State of Legal Research Education: A Survey of First-Year Legal Research Programs, or Why Johnny and Jane Cannot Research. *Law Library Journal, 108*(3), 403-426.

Parise, A. (2010). The 13 Steps of Successful Academic Legal Research. *International Journal of Legal Information, 38*(1), 1-18.

Peoples, L. F. (2005). The Death of the Digest and the Pitfalls of Electronic Research: What Is the Modern Legal Researcher to Do. *Law Librarian Journal, 97*(4), 661-680.

Poincare, H. (1913). *The Foundations of Science: Science and Hypothesis, The Value of Science, Science and Method*: University Press of America.

Posner, R. A. (1993). *The problems of Jurisprudence.* Harvard: Harvard University Press.

Posner, R. A. (2008). The State of Legal Scholarship Today. A Comment on Schlag. *The Georgetown law journal, 67*(3), 845-856.

Posner, R. A. (2010). *Economic Analysis of Law* (3 ed.): Wolters Kluwer.

Rubin, E. L. (1997). Law And and the Methodology of Law. *Wisconsin Law Review, 1997*(3), 521-566.

Rubin, E. L. (2001). Legal Scholarship *International Encyclopedia of the Social & Behavioral Sciences* (pp. 8677-8684).

Rucinski, T. L. (2015). The Elephant in the Room: Toward a Definition of Grey Legal Literature. *Law Library Journal, 107*(4), 543-560.

Samuel, G. (2014). *An Introduction to Comparative Law Theory and Method.* Hart Publishing.

Sandelowski, M., Docherty, S., & Emden, C. (1997). Qualitative metasynthesis: issues and techniques. *Research in Nursing and Health, 20*(4), 365-371.

Scordato, M. R. (2008). Reflections on the Nature of Legal Scholarship in the Post-Realist Era. *Santa Clara Law Review, 48*(2), 353-440.

Siems, M. M. (2008). Legal Originality. *Oxford Journal of Legal Studies, 28*(1), 147-164.

Smith, K. H. (1998). Practical Jurisprudence: Deconstructing and Synthesizing the Art and Science of Thinking Like a Lawyer. *The University of Memphis Law Review, 29*(1), 1-68.

Smits, J. M. (2015). *What is legal doctrine? On the aims and methods of legal-dogmatic research.* Maastricht University. Maastricht.

Snel, M. V. R. (2014). Source-usage within doctrinal legal inquiry: choices, problems and challenges. *Law and Method, 4*(2), 1-22.

Snel, M. V. R. (2016). *Meester(s) over bronnen. Een empirische studie naar kwaliteitseisen, gevaren en onderzoekstechnieken die betrekking hebben op het brongebruik in academisch juridisch-dogmatisch onderzoek.* Den Haag: Boom juridisch.

Snel, M. V. R. (2017a). De 'goede' onderzoeksopzet als succesfactor voor de juridische scriptie. *Ars Aequi, 67*(9), 748-754.

Snel, M. V. R. (2017b). Making the Implicit Quality Standards and Performance Indicators for Traditional Legal Scholarship Explicit. Forthcoming.

Stolker, C. J. J. M. (2014). *Rethinking the Law School - Education, Research, Outreach and Governance.* Cambridge: Cambridge University Press.

Strauss, A. L., & Corbin, J. M. (1998). *Basics of Qualitative Research: Techniques and Procedures for Developing Grounded Theory.* Thousand Oaks: Sage.

Stürner, R. (2012). Das Zivilrecht der Moderne und die Bedeutung der Rechtsdogmatik. *JuristenZeitung, 67*(1), 10-24.

Svacina, S., & Van Gompel, H. (2012). Kwaliteitscontrole en wetenschappelijk uitgeven. In E. Devroe, L. Pauwels, A. Verhage, M. Easton & M. Cools (Eds.), *Tegendraadse criminologie. Liber Amicorum Paul Ponsaers.* Antwerpen/Apeldoorn: Maklu.

Taekema, H. S., & Van Klink, B. M. J. (2011). On the Border. Limits and Possibilities of Interdisciplinary Research. In H. S. Taekema & B. v. Klink (Eds.), *Law and Method. Interdisciplinary Research into Law* (pp. 7-32). Tübingen: Mohr Siebeck.

Thomas, P. A., & Knowles, J. (2006). *Knowles & Thomas: Effective Legal Research.* London: Sweet & Maxwell.

Tijssen, H. E. B. (2009). *De juridische dissertatie onder de loep: de verantwoording van methodologische keuzes in juridische dissertaties.* Amsterdam: Boom Juridische Uitgevers.

Tiller, E., & Cross, F. (2006). What is Legal Doctrine? *Northwestern University Law Review, 100*(1), 517-533.

Tjaden, T. (2010). *Legal research and writing.* Toronto: Irwin Law.

Tjong Tjin Tai, T. F. E. (2013). Verantwoording van bronnen. In G. Van Dijck, R. A. J. Van Gestel, I. Giesen & A. Hammerstein (Eds.), *Cirkels. Een terugblik op een vooruitziende blik* (pp. 201-208). Deventer: Kluwer.

Tjong Tjin Tai, T. F. E. (2017). *Methods of Legal Research.* Reader for educational purposes.

Tsai, D., & Minick, C. (2009). Google Scholar: A New Way to Search for Cases and Related Legal Publications. Retrieved from LLRX website: <www.llrx.com/features/googlescholar.htm>.

Van Dijck, G. (2011). *Kwaliteit van de juridische annotatie. Een empirische studie naar kenmerken en kwaliteitsindicatoren*. Den Haag: Boom Juridische Uitgevers.

Van Dijck, G. (2016). Legal Research When Relying on Open Access: A Primer. *Law and Method, 6*(2), 1-11.

Van Gestel, R. A. J. (2013). Ontspoorde experimenten. *Regelmaat, 28*(1), 59-69.

Van Gestel, R. A. J. (2015). Kwaliteit van juridische publicaties. In P. J. P. M. Van Lochem, R. A. J. Van Gestel & R. H. De Bock (Eds.), *Kwaliteit als keuze: kwaliteit(sbeoordeling) van rechtspraak, wetgeving en rechtswetenschappelijk onderzoek* (pp. 243-378). Den Haag: Wolters Kluwer.

Van Gestel, R. A. J., & Micklitz, H.-W. (2014). Why Methods Matter in European Legal Scholarship. *European Law Journal, 20*(3), 292-316.

Van Gestel, R. A. J., Micklitz, H.-W., & Maduro, M. P. (2012). *Methodology in the New Legal World*. EUI Working Papers Law 2012/13. Florence.

Van Hoecke, M. A. A. (2010). *Is de rechtswetenschap een empirische wetenschap?* Den Haag: Boom Juridische uitgevers.

Van Hoecke, M. A. A. (2015). Methodology of Comparative Legal Research. *Law and Method, 5*(2), 1-35.

Van Leeuwen, T. (2013). Bibliometric research evaluations, Web of Science and the Social Sciences and Humanities: a problematic relationship? *Bibliometrie - Praxis and Forschung, Band* 2, 1-18.

Van Opijnen, M. (2014). *Op en in het web. Hoe de toegankelijkheid van rechterlijke uitspraken kan worden verbeterd*. Den Haag: Boom Juridische Uitgevers.

Verschuren, P. J. M., & Doorewaard, H. A. C. M. (2010). *Designing a Research Project* (Vol. 2). Den Haag: Eleven International Publishing.

Vilaça, G. V. (2015). Why Teach Legal Theory. *German Law Journal, 16*(4), 781-820.

Vranken, J. B. M. (2014). *Mr. C. Asser's Handleiding tot de Beoefening van het Nederlands Burgerlijk Recht: Algemeen deel: Een Synthese*. Deventer: Kluwer.

Wahlgren, P. (2005). The Purpose and Usefulness of Jurisprudence. *Scandinavian Studies in Law, 48*, 505-516.

Westerman, P. (2011). Open or Autonomous? The Debate on Legal Methodology as a Reflection on the Debate on Law. In M. A. A. Van Hoecke (Ed.), *Methodologies of Legal Research. Which Kind of Method for What Kind of Discipline?* (pp. 87-110). Oxford: Hart Publishing.

Westrik, R. 2016). *Verborgen privaatrecht. Hoe het geldende recht te kennen?* Zutphen: Uitgeverij Parijs.

Wisker, G. (2015). Developing doctoral authors: engaging with theoretical perspectives through the literature review. *Innovations in Education and Teaching International, 52*(1), 64-74.

Wissenschaftsrat. (2012). *Perspektiven der Rechtswissenschaft in Deutschlands. Situation, Analysen, Empfehlungen*. Hamburg.

Zuber-Skerritt, O., & Knight, N. (1986). Problem definition and thesis writing. *Higher Education, 15*, 89-103.